Do It Yourself YACHT IMPROVEMENTS

REG MINAL

WATERLINE

With grateful thanks to my wife Francesca for typing
and help in the preparation of this book.

First published in the UK in 1997
by Waterline Books, an imprint of Airlife Publishing Ltd

British Library Cataloguing in Publication Data
A catalogue record for this book
is available from the British Library

ISBN 1 85310 794 8

Typeset by Phoenix Typesetting, Ilkley, West Yorkshire.
Printed in England by Bath Press Ltd., Bath.

Waterline Books
an imprint of Airlife Publishing Ltd
101 Longden Road, Shrewsbury SY3 9EB, England

Preface

There is nothing more satisfying for the do-it-yourself boat owner than to make something for a few coppers that would otherwise cost an 'arm and a leg' at the chandlers.

In this book I have put together a collection of sketches and instructions to construct workable alternatives to otherwise costly equipment required when we put to sea (or river) in small boats and yachts.

Most of the items included have been tried and tested, and many are in everyday use on my own home-built ferro-cement yacht *Concrete Evidence*.

Some of these ideas have been adapted from articles and tips found in yachting magazines, and a few have been invented out of sheer necessity. All of the items can be made fairly easily using simple tools (with one or two exceptions where a small amount of welding will be necessary) and often utilizing scrap material salvaged from the marina rubbish skip.

All dimensions are in millimetres unless otherwise indicated.

R.M.

Contents

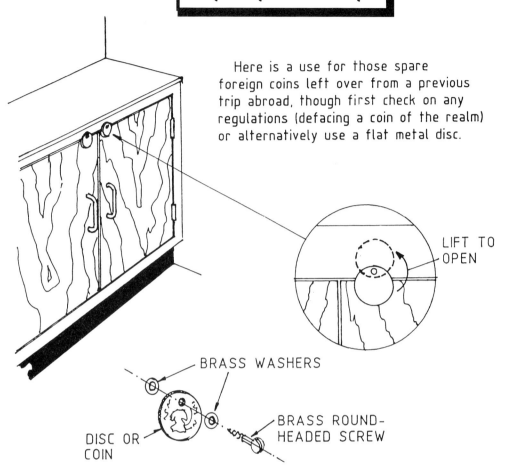

Here is a use for those spare foreign coins left over from a previous trip abroad, though first check on any regulations (defacing a coin of the realm) or alternatively use a flat metal disc.

LIFT TO OPEN

BRASS WASHERS

BRASS ROUND-HEADED SCREW

DISC OR COIN

This catch is easily lifted with the finger and will drop back into place when released. It will keep the cupboard door securely closed in all weathers.

Drill the coin or disc to one side (off centre) and make sure that the screw is quite a loose fit. Assemble with brass washers as shown. Do not tighten screw but leave enough slack to allow the disc to swing freely.

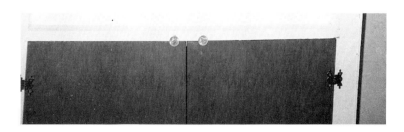

Danbuoy

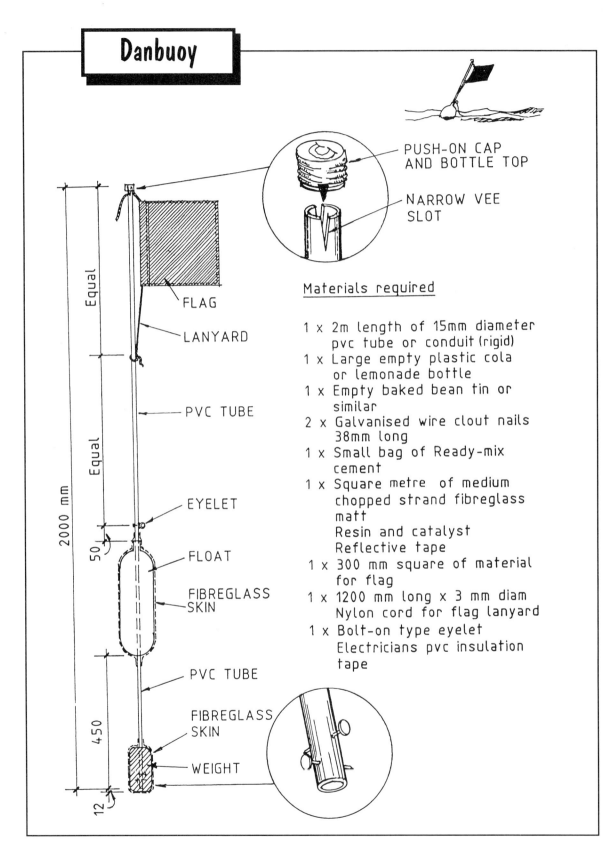

PUSH-ON CAP
AND BOTTLE TOP

NARROW VEE
SLOT

FLAG

LANYARD

PVC TUBE

EYELET

FLOAT

FIBREGLASS
SKIN

PVC TUBE

FIBREGLASS
SKIN

WEIGHT

Equal

Equal

2000 mm

50

450

12

Materials required

1 x 2m length of 15mm diameter
     pvc tube or conduit (rigid)
1 x Large empty plastic cola
     or lemonade bottle
1 x Empty baked bean tin or
     similar
2 x Galvanised wire clout nails
     38mm long
1 x Small bag of Ready-mix
     cement
1 x Square metre of medium
     chopped strand fibreglass
     matt
     Resin and catalyst
     Reflective tape
1 x 300 mm square of material
     for flag
1 x 1200 mm long x 3 mm diam
     Nylon cord for flag lanyard
1 x Bolt-on type eyelet
     Electricians pvc insulation
     tape

Danbuoy

Construction

Cut the top from the plastic bottle, carefully remove the base and cut a hole in the bottom to suit the outside diameter of the tube. Pass the tube through the bottle leaving 450 mm protruding below, and fix in position with electrician's tape.

Using a bradawl, make two holes through the tube, one 30 mm up from the bottom and one 50 mm up from the bottom, the second angled at 90° to the first. Push the two nails through these holes so that they protrude on either side. Position the empty tin with the open top uppermost and place the bottom end of the tube centrally into the can. Tie or wedge it in position about 12 mm above the bottom of the can. Mix the sand and cement and pour into the can, tamping the mixture well down with a small stick. Allow to dry.

When completely dry snip the top of the rim of the can in about six places and using pliers peel back the can and remove. This should leave a can-shaped weight secured to the lower end of the tube. Round the sharp edges with glasspaper.

Cut the chopped-strand glass matt into strips and completely cover the weight and float with fibreglass and resin. Continue the glass along the tube for about 25 mm. When the fibreglass is dry drill a 4 mm diameter hole in the tube approximately 50 mm above the top of the float, and another half-way between this position and the top of the tube. Fix the eyelet bolt in the lower hole. Cut a narrow vee-shaped slot in the top of the tube.

Give a second coat of resin to the float and weight, and when dry lightly sand with fine glasspaper. Apply two coats of gloss paint of the colour of your choice.

Flag

Hem (by hand or machine) the material on three sides to form the flag, double-fold and hem the fourth side, leaving a 12 mm gap for the insertion of the lanyard. Thread the nylon cord through the flag hem and secure the bottom end by tying through the middle hole. Pass the lanyard over the top of the tube and wedge into the vee groove. Place the cut-off bottle top on the top of the tube to secure.

To finish, cut the reflective tape into narrow strips and stick to the sides of upper float and tube. The eyelet bolt is for the attachment of the life buoy lanyard. A flashing strobe light can be attached to the top of the tube, if desired. I fixed a simple battery-powered device purchased from a cycle shop for about one third of the cost of an automatic light from the chandler.

Danbuoy Bracket

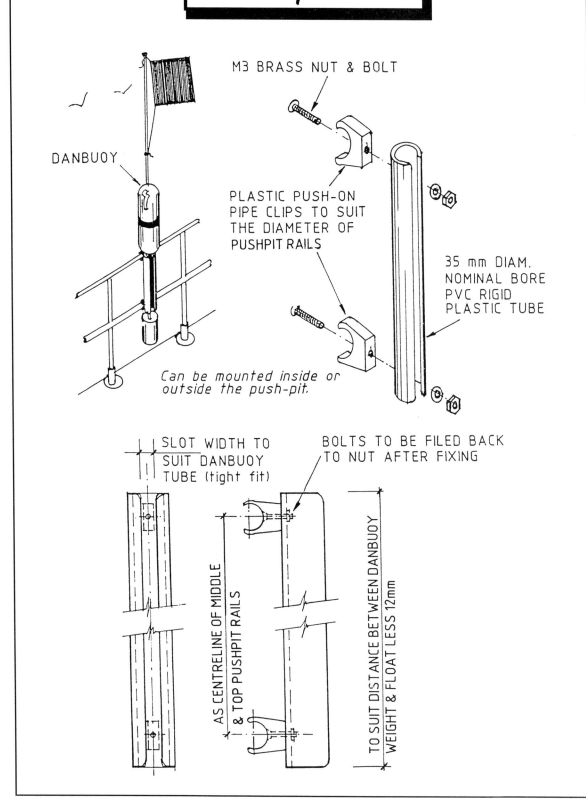

M3 BRASS NUT & BOLT

DANBUOY

PLASTIC PUSH-ON
PIPE CLIPS TO SUIT
THE DIAMETER OF
PUSHPIT RAILS

35 mm DIAM.
NOMINAL BORE
PVC RIGID
PLASTIC TUBE

Can be mounted inside or
outside the push-pit.

SLOT WIDTH TO
SUIT DANBUOY
TUBE (tight fit)

BOLTS TO BE FILED BACK
TO NUT AFTER FIXING

AS CENTRELINE OF MIDDLE
& TOP PUSHPIT RAILS

TO SUIT DISTANCE BETWEEN DANBUOY
WEIGHT & FLOAT LESS 12mm

Danbuoy Bracket

Materials required

1 × length 35 mm diameter Rigid PVC Tube, 450 mm long
2 × Plastic Push-on Pipe Clips, size to suit the outside diameter of your pushpit rails
2 × M3 Brass Countersunk Machine Bolts, 30 mm long (to be cut to length required), with Nuts and Washers

Construction

Cut the tube to required length, i.e. the distance between the top of the danbuoy weight and the bottom of the float less 12 mm.

Carefully measure the outside diameter of the lower danbuoy tube and cut a slot vertically down the tube (this is easily cut with a small tenon saw). Round the edges with a file or glasspaper so that there are no rough edges, and ensure the danbuoy fits in the slot fairly tightly.

Next measure from the centreline of the top pushpit rail to the centreline of the next rail. Mark this carefully on the back of the tube and drill a 4 mm diameter hole in each position. Bolt the push-on clips through the back of the tube as shown. With a round file, file off the end of the bolts so that they do not protrude inside the tube more than is necessary to secure the nuts.

The bracket should now just clip onto the pushpit.

Note

When removing the danbuoy from the bracket, if there is a tendency to pull the bracket away from the pushpit rails the slot is too tight. Widen the slot lightly using a file, until you can remove the danbuoy and leave the bracket in place.

A Cheap Inclinometer

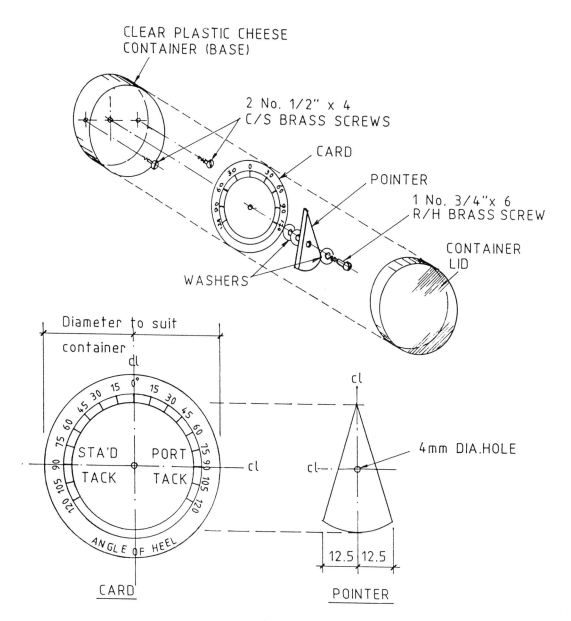

CLEAR PLASTIC CHEESE
CONTAINER (BASE)

2 No. 1/2" x 4
C/S BRASS SCREWS

CARD

POINTER

1 No. 3/4"x 6
R/H BRASS SCREW

CONTAINER
LID

WASHERS

Diameter to suit
container

dl

0°
15 15
30 30
45 45
60 60
75 75
90 STA'D   PORT 90
105 TACK   TACK 105
120   120

cl

ANGLE OF HEEL

CARD

cl

cl   cl

4mm DIA.HOLE

12.5 | 12.5

POINTER

The card shown is for viewing towards the bow. If
the card is for viewing towards the stern, then the
words 'STA'D' and 'PORT' will need to be changed over.

A Cheap Inclinometer

Materials required

1 × small Round Clear Plastic Cheese Container or equivalent
2 × No 4 Brass Countersunk Screws, ½ inch long
1 × No 6 Brass Roundhead Screw, ¾ inch long
1 × small piece Plastic, Aluminium or Brass, approximately 3 mm × 25 mm × 50 mm
3 × M4 Brass Washers
1 × small piece Paper or Card, 100 mm × 100 mm, or Stick-on Compass Rose

Construction

Carefully remove any paper stickers from the container and clean all surfaces with warm water. Drill the holes in the base as shown and fix to bulkhead in an upright position using the two 1/2 inch long No 4 screws in the outer two holes. When drilling take care not to use excessive pressure or the plastic container may shatter.

Using a protractor, mark up the card or paper in degrees or alternatively photocopy the example illustrated (enlarge or reduce as required) and cut out to fit internally in the container. The card can be made using a plastic stick-on compass rose stuck to the card.

Glue the card into the container making sure that the '0°' mark is at the top.

From the small piece of plastic, aluminium or brass, cut out and shape the triangular pointer and drill a 4 mm diameter hole in the centre. Remove all rough edges with glasspaper or a file.

Assemble using the 3/4" long No. 6 screw and the washers as indicated, being careful not to tighten the screw fully, to enable the pointer to swing freely. Finally, replace the container cover to complete.

A Cheap Inclinometer.

Inexpensive Cockpit Lockers

self-draining~

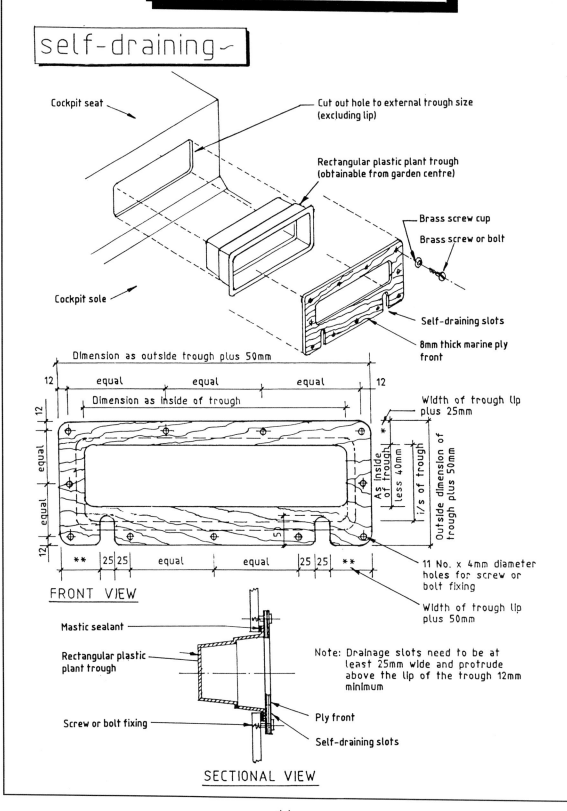

Cockpit seat

Cut out hole to external trough size (excluding lip)

Rectangular plastic plant trough (obtainable from garden centre)

Brass screw cup

Brass screw or bolt

Cockpit sole

Self-draining slots

8mm thick marine ply front

Dimension as outside trough plus 50mm

12 | equal | equal | equal | 12

Dimension as inside of trough

Width of trough lip plus 25mm

12

equal

equal

12

As inside of trough less 40mm

i/s of trough

Outside dimension of trough plus 50mm

25 25 | equal | equal | 25 25

11 No. x 4mm diameter holes for screw or bolt fixing

FRONT VIEW

Width of trough lip plus 50mm

Mastic sealant

Rectangular plastic plant trough

Screw or bolt fixing

Note: Drainage slots need to be at least 25mm wide and protrude above the lip of the trough 12mm minimum

Ply front

Self-draining slots

SECTIONAL VIEW

Inexpensive Cockpit Lockers

Materials required

1 × Rectangular Plastic Plant Trough (obtainable from garden centres or gardening shops). They come in a variety of sizes, usually 120 mm to 150 mm wide × 400 mm to 800 mm long
1 × piece 8 mm Marine or Weatherproof Plywood, 50 mm wider × 50 mm longer than plant trough
11 × No 6 Brass Screws or Nuts and Bolts, with Brass Screw Cups or Washers. You may require more if a large trough is used

Construction

Measure the outside top of the plant trough less the lip and mark this out on any convenient bulkhead, cockpit side etc. where you wish to position your locker. Cut out the hole allowing for any rounded corners and ensure that the trough fits the opening with the lip resting on the cut-out edge.

Next mark and cut out the front panel as shown and drill holes for screw or bolt fixings. Sand, varnish or paint both sides and the edges.

Apply a generous bead of mastic sealant (*Sikaflex* or similar) to the underside of the trough lip. Press into position in the cut-out. Next position the front panel so that the inside top and sides line up with the inside of the trough. Screw or bolt together, sandwiching the lip of the trough between the structure and the front panel.

The low upstand of the ply panel prevents objects falling out of the locker.

Even More Inexpensive Cockpit Lockers

self-draining

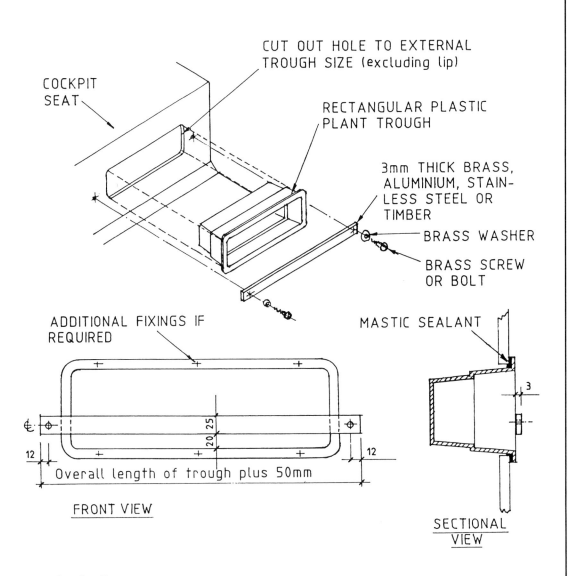

CUT OUT HOLE TO EXTERNAL TROUGH SIZE (excluding lip)

COCKPIT SEAT

RECTANGULAR PLASTIC PLANT TROUGH

3mm THICK BRASS, ALUMINIUM, STAINLESS STEEL OR TIMBER

BRASS WASHER

BRASS SCREW OR BOLT

ADDITIONAL FIXINGS IF REQUIRED

MASTIC SEALANT

Overall length of trough plus 50mm

FRONT VIEW

SECTIONAL VIEW

Construction.

Cut out the bulkhead and fit the plant trough as described in previous pages.
Cut the 25mm x 3mm thick brass, aluminium, or stainless steel flat bar or timber batten to overlap the length of the trough by 25mm on each side. Drill a 4mm diameter hole on the centre line and 12mm in from each end for screw or bolt fixing. Assemble using a mastic-type sealant between the plant trough lip and the bulkhead or coaming.
Use additional screw fixings through the lip of the trough if required.

Fender Adjuster

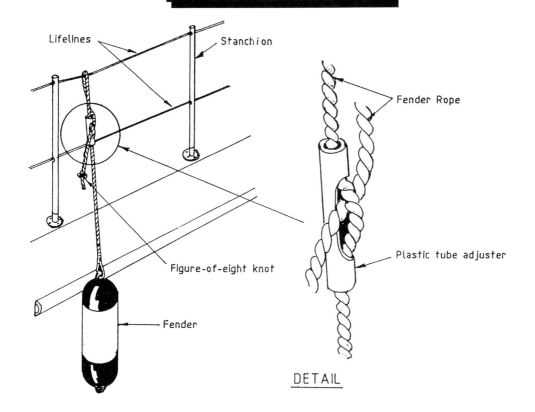

Lifelines

Stanchion

Fender Rope

Figure-of-eight knot

Plastic tube adjuster

Fender

DETAIL

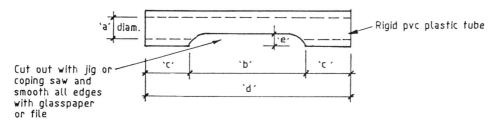

'a' diam.

Rigid pvc plastic tube

'e'

'c' 'b' 'c'

Cut out with jig or
coping saw and
smooth all edges
with glasspaper
or file

'd'

DIMENSIONS					
Rope size diameter	a	b	c	d	e
6 to 8mm	10mm	40mm	15mm	70mm	5mm
10 to 12mm	13mm	50mm	15mm	80mm	6mm
13 to 19mm	20mm	60mm	17mm	94mm	9mm

Each adjuster is cut from
rigid pvc plastic tube (water
grade) obtainable from D.I.Y.
stores in 2 metre lengths.

The tube adjuster is threaded onto the fender rope, the rope is passed around the
lifeline or stanchion, then with the thumb and forefinger pull a loop of rope out from
the slot and thread the free end of the rope through this. By sliding the adjuster up
or down height adjustment is easily made. A figure-of-eight knot in the free end of
the rope will prevent nylon ropes slipping through, saving the possible loss of the fender.

Simple Derrick

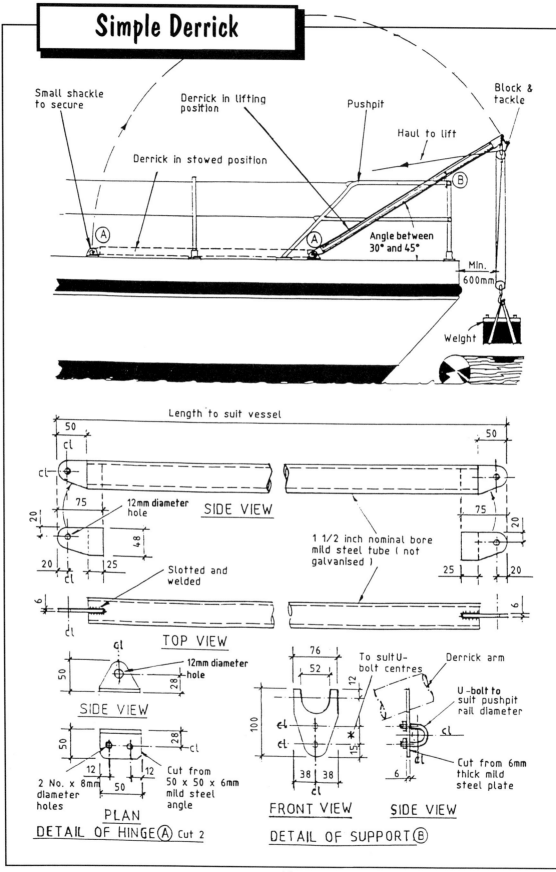

Small shackle to secure

Derrick in lifting position

Pushpit

Haul to lift

Block & tackle

Derrick in stowed position

Angle between 30° and 45°

Min. 600mm

Weight

Length to suit vessel

50

cl

cl

75

12mm diameter hole

SIDE VIEW

50

75

1 1/2 inch nominal bore mild steel tube (not galvanised)

20

48

20   25

25   20

6   6

Slotted and welded

cl

TOP VIEW

cl

12mm diameter hole

50

28

SIDE VIEW

50   28

cl

12   12

2 No. x 8mm diameter holes   50   Cut from 50 x 50 x 6mm mild steel angle

PLAN

DETAIL OF HINGE Ⓐ Cut 2

76

52   12

To suit U-bolt centres

Derrick arm

100

cl

cl

15

U-bolt to suit pushpit rail diameter

38   38

6

Cut from 6mm thick mild steel plate

cl

FRONT VIEW   SIDE VIEW

DETAIL OF SUPPORT Ⓑ

Simple Derrick

Materials required

1 × length 1½ inch nominal bore Black Mild Steel Tube, length to suit vessel. 1½ inch nominal bore tube has an outside diameter of approximately 48 mm
2 × pieces Mild Steel Plate, 6 mm × 48 mm × 75 mm
1 × piece Mild Steel Plate, 6 mm × 76 mm × 100 mm
2 × pieces Mild Steel Angle, 6 mm × 50 mm × 50 mm
1 × Galvanised or Stainless Steel U-Bolt, diameter to suit pushpit rail, with Nuts
4 × M6 Bolts, Nuts and Washers for bolting down hinges, length to suit deck thickness
1 × M12 Hexagon Bolt, 30 mm long, with Nut, Locking Nut and Washers
1 × small Galvanised or Stainless Steel Shackle

Construction

Decide on a suitable position to mount your derrick on the deck and measure length required. Cut and drill the two small plates to fit into the ends of the tube. Cut slots in the tube at each end using a drill and hacksaw and weld the plates into the tube ends as shown.

Next shape and drill the two angle hinges (A) and position on the deck as shown in the sketch. The position of the hinge nearest the stern will determine the angle of the derrick. Drill through the deck and fix this one first. You may wish to fit a backing plate under the deck to prevent the bolts being pulled up through the deck if lifting very heavy weights.

Bolt the inboard end of the tube to the hinge using the nut and locknut and swing the tube inboard, to determine the position for fixing the second hinge (this is not really a hinge but is similar to the first). Bolt this down to the deck. A backing plate should not be necessary for this.

Next cut, drill and shape the plate support (B) and assemble over the top rail of your pushpit using the U-bolt. Check the position on the rail is correct for supporting the tube and tighten the nuts on the U-bolt.

The whole derrick should be galvanised or painted with *Galvafroid* or *Hammerite* paint.

When not in use the tube will swing over and lie flat on the deck, the end secured with a shackle. This can be the same shackle used to attach the block and tackle arrangement.

Note

Should you decide to use galvanised instead of black tube, the galvanising must be removed in the area of the weld as welding galvanised metal produces toxic fumes.

A Simple Derrick

A Foldaway Seat

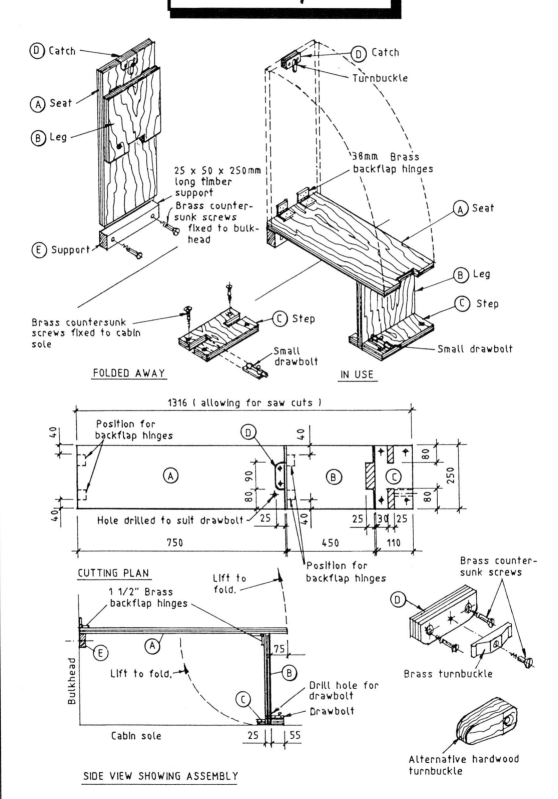

D Catch

A Seat

B Leg

25 x 50 x 250mm long timber support
Brass counter-sunk screws fixed to bulkhead

E Support

Brass countersunk screws fixed to cabin sole

C Step

Small drawbolt

FOLDED AWAY

D Catch

Turnbuckle

38mm Brass backflap hinges

A Seat

B Leg

C Step

Small drawbolt

IN USE

1316 (allowing for saw cuts)

Position for backflap hinges

40

D

40

A

80 90

B

C

80

250

80

Hole drilled to suit drawbolt   25   40   25   30   25

750   450   110

CUTTING PLAN

Position for backflap hinges

1 1/2" Brass backflap hinges

Lift to fold.

Bulkhead

E

A

Lift to fold,

B

C

75

Drill hole for drawbolt

Drawbolt

Cabin sole   25   55

SIDE VIEW SHOWING ASSEMBLY

Brass counter-sunk screws

D

Brass turnbuckle

Alternative hardwood turnbuckle

A Foldaway Seat

Materials required

1 × piece 25 mm Marine or Weatherproof Plywood, 250 mm × 1316 mm
4 × Brass Backflap Hinges, 38 mm or 1½ inch wide, with Brass Screws
1 × small Brass Drawbolt, 50 mm long maximum, with Brass Screws
1 × Brass Turnbuckle or make one from timber
1 × Timber Batten, 25 mm × 50 mm × 250 mm
2 × No 12 Brass Countersunk Screws for fixing support (E), length to suit
7 × Brass Countersunk Screws for fixing step (C) and catch (D), length to suit

Construction

Mark the plywood as shown in the cutting plan and cut into the three major components (A), (B) and (C). Using a coping saw or jigsaw, carefully cut out part D from Part A. Then cut the slots as shown for parts B and C. Make sure part B fits into the slots in part C (not too tightly).

Assemble in position on your boat as shown using the hinges. The top backflap hinges can be set flush into the seat for a neater finish if desired, but this is not essential.

Then fix the catch piece (D) with the turnbuckle and fit the brass drawbolt to part C. This will need a small hole drilled through the leg (B) into which the drawbolt can slide, making the seat secure in rough weather.

Finally, with the seat in the lowered position fix the support (E). This support is essential if you don't wish to finish up sitting on the floor as the hinges alone will not support your weight. To finish, sand and varnish or paint as you desire.

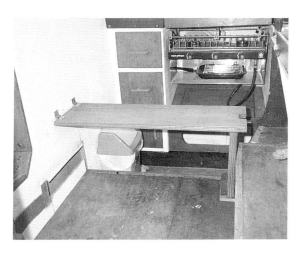

A Foldaway Seat

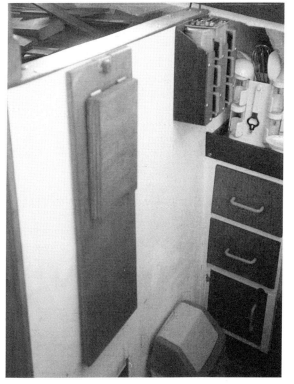

Water Tank Gauge

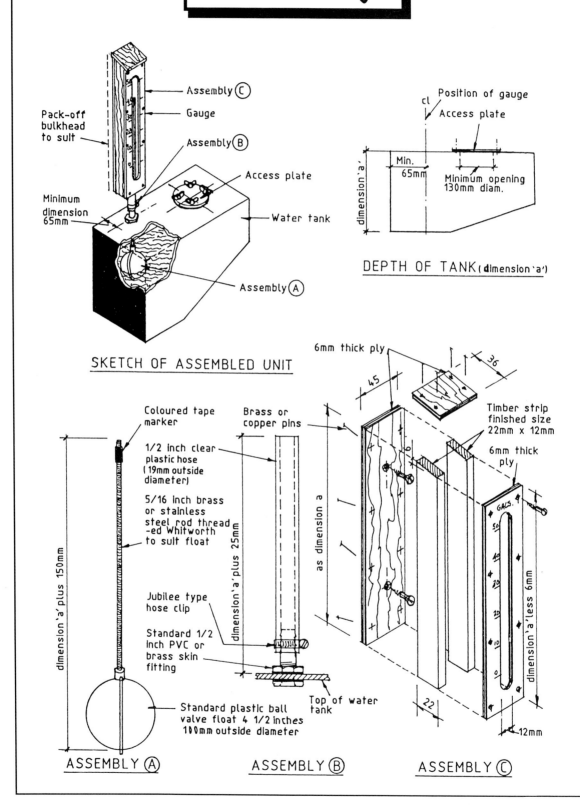

SKETCH OF ASSEMBLED UNIT

Assembly (C)
Gauge
Pack-off bulkhead to suit
Assembly (B)
Access plate
Minimum dimension 65mm
Water tank
Assembly (A)

Position of gauge
cl
Access plate
dimension 'a'
Min. 65mm
Minimum opening 130mm diam.

DEPTH OF TANK (dimension 'a')

Coloured tape marker
1/2 inch clear plastic hose (19mm outside diameter)
5/16 inch brass or stainless steel rod threaded Whitworth to suit float
dimension 'a' plus 150mm
Jubilee type hose clip
Standard 1/2 inch PVC or brass skin fitting
Standard plastic ball valve float 4 1/2 inches 100mm outside diameter

ASSEMBLY (A)

Brass or copper pins
dimension 'a' plus 25mm
Top of water tank

ASSEMBLY (B)

6mm thick ply
45
36
Timber strip finished size 22mm x 12mm
6mm thick ply
as dimension a
GALS.
22
dimension 'a' less 6mm
12mm

ASSEMBLY (C)

Water Tank Gauge

This gauge is only suitable for water tanks and must not be used for fuel tanks.

Materials required

1 × Standard Plastic Ball Valve Float, 112 mm (4½ inch) diameter
1 × length 5/16 inch Brass or Stainless Steel Whitworth Threaded Rod, for length see sketch
1 × 12.5 mm (½ inch) Brass or Plastic Skin Fitting for hose connection, with Backnut and Washer
1 × length 12.5 mm (½ inch) internal diameter Clear Plastic Hose, for length see sketch. This has an outside diameter of 19 mm
1 × Jubilee Hose Clip to suit plastic hose
2 × pieces Planed Timber, 12 mm × 22 mm (finished size), for length see sketch
1 × piece 6 mm Marine or Weatherproof Plywood, 45 mm wide, for length see sketch
8 × No 4 Brass Roundhead Screws, 12.5 mm (½ inch) long
2 × No 6 Brass Countersunk Screws, 19 mm (¾ inch) long
12 × Brass or Copper Panel Pins, 18 mm long
1 × small piece Brightly Coloured Electrician's Tape

Construction

First check that your tank has a suitable access plate with an opening of at least 130 mm diameter. If your tank does not have one then you will have to fit one before installing this type of gauge.

Drill a 19 mm diameter hole in the top of your tank at least 65 mm from any side and close to a bulkhead or partition. Install the skin fitting from inside the tank, with the backnut on the outside and the hose connection looking upwards (see assembly B).

Push the ball float inside the tank and push the rod down through the skin fitting. Putting your hand inside the access hole in the tank manipulate the ball under the skin fitting and screw in the threaded rod (see assembly A). Next, fit the clear hosepipe over the skin fitting and the rod and secure to the skin fitting with the hose clip.

Cut the plywood into three pieces as shown in the sketch, and assemble the timber sides and the ply back and top (see assembly C). Place this around the tube and mark the position on the adjacent bulkhead, using packing timber behind the gauge to ensure that the plastic hose is not distorted.

Undo the clip and remove the plastic hose by pulling forward. Stick the electrician's tape around the threaded rod so that the tape marker rests a little way up from the bottom of the gauge when empty.

Fix the packing strips and screw assembly C, without the front panel, in position and re-fix the plastic hose and clip. Finally, screw on the front panel. Make sure that when the ball float is raised inside the tank the rod with its marker rises freely up the tube. Varnish or paint assembly C to finish.

Calibration

Mark the empty or zero position on the panel. Using a suitable measure like a two-gallon bucket, fill the tank to where you want your first calibration mark, say at 10 gallons. Make a mark on the front panel and continue marking at 10-gallon intervals until the tank is full. These marks can be squared across the front panel, and scored or marked with felt tip pen.

Wall-Hung Cup Rack

CUP OR MUG DIMENSIONS

Your own cup or mug dimensions

a	mm	b	mm	c	mm	d	mm

Stack cups upside down to drain

ASSEMBLED UNIT

FRONT VIEW

12 ⌐ 'a' + 3 ⌐ 'a' + 3 ⌐ 12

12

$(3 \times b) + a + 12mm$

12

12

'd' + 2 ⌐ 'd' + 2

$(2 \times 'a') + 30$

Base

SIDE VIEW

12

12

6 ⌐ 'a' + 3 ⌐ 6

Back 6mm thick ply

Brass fixing screws to bulkhead

6 mm thick ply fronts

3/4 inch x No.4 brass countersunk wood screws with brass screw cups

Copper or brass panel pins

Timber battens finished size 12mm x 'a'+3mm

DETAIL OF JOINT AT BASE

12

6

Base

EXPLODED VIEW

This rack is designed for 6 cups or mugs, however dimensions can be modified for 4,8 or 12 cups if desired.

Wall-Hung Cup Rack

Materials required

1 × piece 6 mm Marine or Weatherproof Plywood, for dimensions see sketch
1 × piece Planed Timber, 12 mm thick, for width and length see sketch
10 × No 4 Brass Countersunk Wood Screws, 18 mm long, with Brass Screw Cups
2 × Brass Countersunk Wood Screws for fixing to bulkhead
17 × Brass or Copper Panel Pins, 18 mm long

Construction

First, purchase your stacking mugs or cups and measure the outside diameter (a), the heights (b) and (c) and the width of the handle (d). Mark these on the sketch for reference.

Using the drawing cut your timber and ply to size. The dimensions are shown on the sketch thus: 'a + 3' means measurement 'a' plus 3 mm; '(3 × b) + a + 12' means three times measurement 'b' plus measurement 'a' plus 12 mm.

Cut the base halving joints and glue and pin this section first. Next, fit the back, making sure it is square, and glue and pin in position. Finally, screw the three front panels in position. Using a pin punch, tap the pin heads below the surface and fill with wood stopper. Sand down and varnish.

Note

If using brass pins pre-drill small holes as otherwise you will find these pins, being soft, will bend over. By toshing the pins (i.e. angling them slightly, see sketch) you will make a much stronger joint.

A Wall-Hung Cup Rack

Companionway Cover

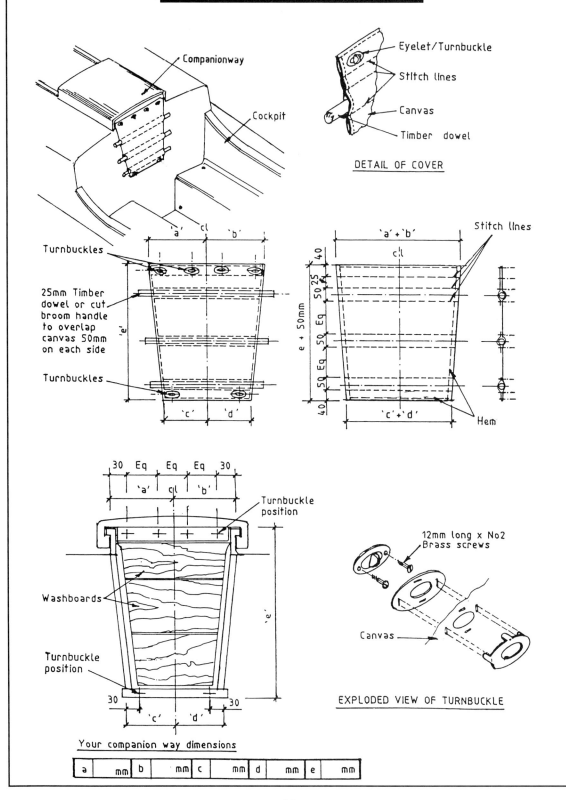

Companionway

Cockpit

Eyelet/Turnbuckle

Stitch lines

Canvas

Timber dowel

DETAIL OF COVER

Turnbuckles

25mm Timber dowel or cut broom handle to overlap canvas 50mm on each side

Turnbuckles

Stitch lines

Hem

Washboards

Turnbuckle position

Turnbuckle position

12mm long x No2 Brass screws

Canvas

EXPLODED VIEW OF TURNBUCKLE

Your companion way dimensions

a	mm	b	mm	c	mm	d	mm	e	mm

Companionway Cover

Materials required

1 × piece Medium or Heavy Grade Canvas, ('a' + 'b' + 20 mm) × ('e' + 'e' + 120mm). To calculate size see sketch
6 × small Brass or Plated Turnbuttons/ Turnbuckles for fixing to wood or GRP, with Eyelets
12 × No 2 Brass Screws, 12 mm long
3 × lengths 25 mm diameter Timber Dowel or Broom Handle, for length see sketch
Sewing Twine or Cotton

Construction

Carefully measure the dimensions ('a' to 'e') of your companionway and note these measurements in the boxes provided on the sketch. Fold the canvas in half, with the fold at the top, and mark out the shape with top 'a + b', sides 'e + 50 mm' and bottom 'c + d'. Allow an additional 10 mm on the sides and bottom to allow for hemming the edge. Unfold and, using a sewing machine or by hand, form and stitch the hem all the way round.

Re-fold and mark the positions for the dowels on one side only, then machine stitch or hand sew along the stitch lines shown on the sketch. Ensure that the dowel can be pushed through the pocket between the stitch lines. Cut the dowel to length for each pocket, allowing it to project approximately 50 mm on each side.

Next, fix the eyelets of the turnbuckles in position on the cover, as indicated in the sketch.

Position the cover over the companionway and, using a pencil, mark through the eyelets on to the companionway surround. Fix the turnbuckles to the surround with the screws.

The cover is used when sailing with the washboards removed, to prevent spray entering the cabin. It can be quickly pushed aside for entry or exit to the cabin below. The dowels prevent the wind from lifting the canvas cover. Normally only the top turnbuckles are used to keep the cover in place.

It is stressed that this cover is to prevent the ingress of spray or rain only and is not meant to replace the washboards in rough weather.

Companionway Cover

27

and DRAIN CLEARERS

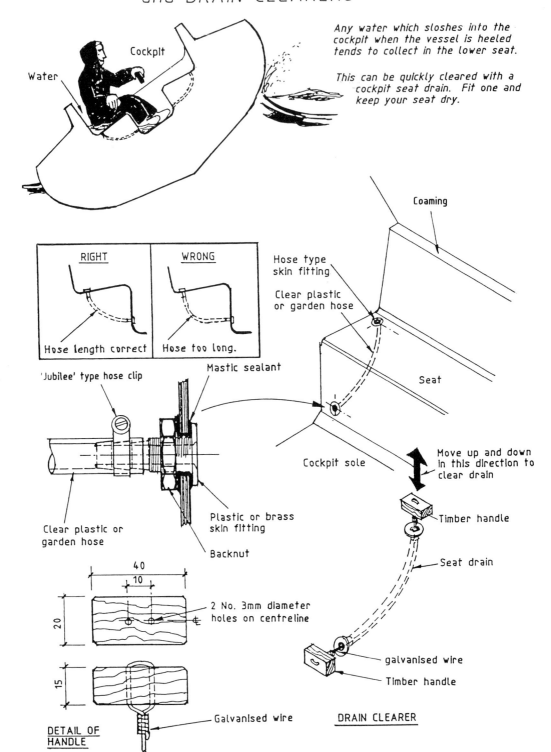

Any water which sloshes into the cockpit when the vessel is heeled tends to collect in the lower seat.

This can be quickly cleared with a cockpit seat drain. Fit one and keep your seat dry.

Water

Cockpit

Coaming

Hose type skin fitting

Clear plastic or garden hose

Seat

RIGHT	WRONG
Hose length correct	Hose too long.

Cockpit sole

Move up and down in this direction to clear drain

'Jubilee' type hose clip

Mastic sealant

Timber handle

Clear plastic or garden hose

Plastic or brass skin fitting

Backnut

Seat drain

40

10

20

2 No. 3mm diameter holes on centreline

galvanised wire

Timber handle

15

Galvanised wire

DETAIL OF HANDLE

DRAIN CLEARER

Cockpit Seat Drains

Materials required

For each drain:
2 × Brass or Plastic Skin Fittings for hose connection, with Backnuts, the bigger the better (within practical limits)
1 × length Clear PVC Hose or Garden Hose to suit skin fittings
2 × Jubilee Hose Clips to suit hose

For each drain clearer:
1 × length 2 mm or 3 mm Rigid Galvanised Wire or unravel an old wire coat hanger
2 × small Hardwood Blocks, 15 mm × 20 mm × 40 mm (dimensions are not critical)

Construction

Measure the outside thread size of your skin fittings, and mark your hole positions in the seat and seat side. Check that there are no bearers on the inside or other obstructions. Using a brace and bit, cut the holes. Fit the skin fittings in position with the hose connection on the inside, using a suitable weatherproof sealant. Cut and fix the hoses with the hose clips. It is important to keep the hose lengths fairly short, otherwise water will lie in the pipes and this could cause leaks.

Drain clearer

In port or in the boatyard drains frequently get blocked with debris. These drain cleaners are a quick and efficient method of removing this and well worth fitting.

First cut the timber handles, which can be made from any small scrap of hardwood. Remove any burrs or sharp corners with glasspaper and drill two 3 mm diameter holes about 10 mm apart in each block as shown on sketch.

Thread the galvanised wire through the holes of one handle only. Twist up tight with a pair of pliers as shown on the sketch. Next thread the loose end through the drain and fix the other handle as before, making sure that the completed drain clearer is 50 to 100 mm longer than the drain. Paint or varnish handles to complete.

Step Locker

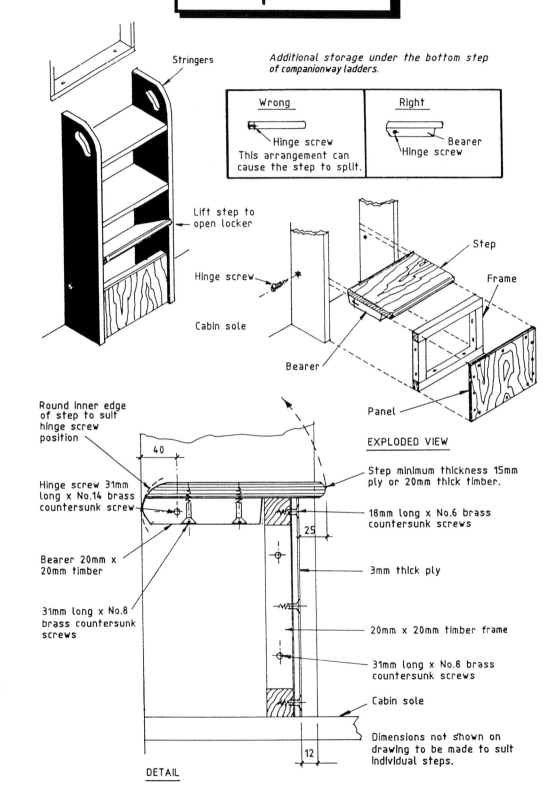

Stringers

Additional storage under the bottom step of companionway ladders.

Wrong	Right
Hinge screw	Bearer
This arrangement can cause the step to split.	Hinge screw

Lift step to open locker

Hinge screw

Cabin sole

Step

Frame

Bearer

Panel

EXPLODED VIEW

Round inner edge of step to suit hinge screw position

Hinge screw 31mm long x No.14 brass countersunk screw

Bearer 20mm x 20mm timber

31mm long x No.8 brass countersunk screws

Step minimum thickness 15mm ply or 20mm thick timber.

18mm long x No.6 brass countersunk screws

3mm thick ply

20mm x 20mm timber frame

31mm long x No.8 brass countersunk screws

Cabin sole

Dimensions not shown on drawing to be made to suit individual steps.

DETAIL

Step Locker

Materials required

1 × piece Timber, 20 mm × 20 mm (finished size), cut into lengths to suit existing step
1 × piece 15 mm Marine or Weatherproof Plywood or 20 mm thick Timber, size to suit existing tread
1 × piece 3 mm Marine or Weatherproof Plywood, size to suit height and width of existing step
12 × No 6 Brass Countersunk Screws, 18 mm long
10 × No 8 Brass Countersunk Screws, 31 mm long
2 × No 14 Brass Countersunk Screws, 31 mm long
2 × 6 mm diameter Brass or Stainless Steel Washers

Construction

Remove the bottom tread from existing companionway steps. If it is recessed into the stringers, you will need to fill in the recesses.

Cut and fit the front panel. Then cut two pieces of 20 mm × 20 mm timber the width of the panel and screw in position to the panel (top and bottom). Cut two more pieces and fill in the ends. Drill the frame (bottom and sides only) and screw into position as shown on the sketch, inset 12 mm from the front face of the stringers. Cut and fit the step/lid (this should be a loose fit) and fix the two bearers on each side. Round the front and also the rear of the step, so that when the step is raised it will not bind on the bulkhead. Carefully measure the position for the hinge screw, and drill on each side. Before assembly, slip washers onto the screws between the stringers and bearers. Do not overtighten the screws. Paint or varnish to complete.

Bosun's Chair

BROADEN YOUR HORIZON WITH A BOSUNS CHAIR.

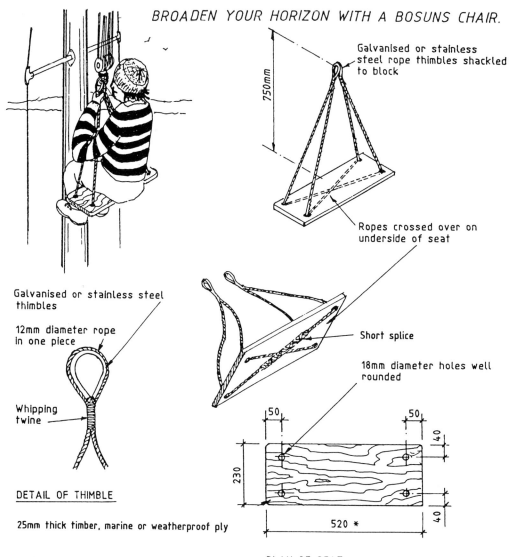

750mm

Galvanised or stainless steel rope thimbles shackled to block

Ropes crossed over on underside of seat

Galvanised or stainless steel thimbles

12mm diameter rope in one piece

Whipping twine

Short splice

18mm diameter holes well rounded

DETAIL OF THIMBLE

25mm thick timber, marine or weatherproof ply

50   50

40

230

40

520 *

PLAN OF SEAT

Materials required

1 piece of timber, marine or weatherproof ply, size 520mm long x 230mm wide x 25mm thick
1 piece of 12mm diameter three strand rope, 5 metres long
2 x galvanised or stainless steel rope thimbles, to suit 12mm diameter rope
Waxed whipping twine

Note: For extra large crew members, dimension * 520 may need to be increased.

Construction

Cut the seat to size and drill the four holes to take the ropes. Make sure these holes are smooth and well rounded to prevent chafe. Thread the rope through the holes as indicated above and join with short splice on the underside of the seat. The rope must cross underneath to give maximum adjustment. Arrange the short splice centrally between the diagonal holes, and tape the thimbles in position at the highest point. Check that the two thimbles come together centrally and at a point approximately 750mm above the seat. Whip the rope together for about 50mm below each thimble. The two thimbles are shackled together and to the lifting block.

Rope Box/ Bridge Deck

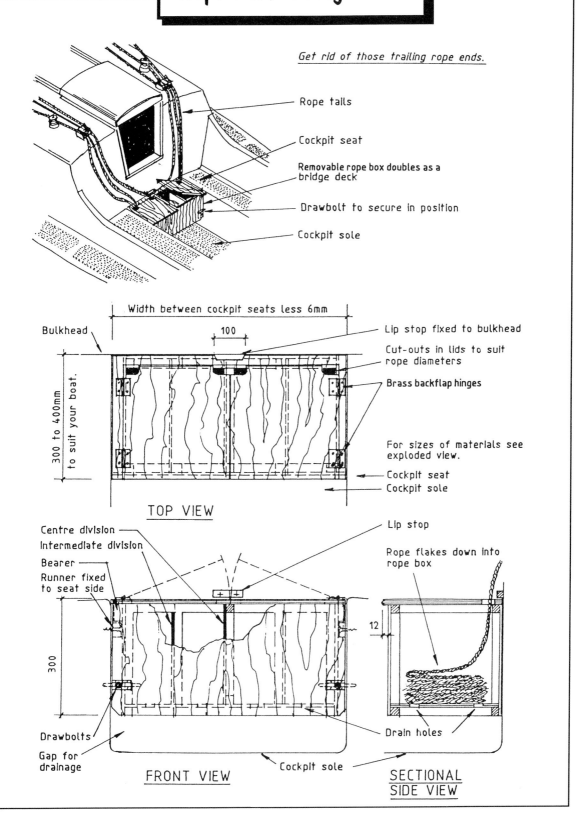

Get rid of those trailing rope ends.

Rope tails

Cockpit seat

Removable rope box doubles as a bridge deck

Drawbolt to secure in position

Cockpit sole

Width between cockpit seats less 6mm

100

Bulkhead

300 to 400mm to suit your boat.

Lip stop fixed to bulkhead

Cut-outs in lids to suit rope diameters

Brass backflap hinges

For sizes of materials see exploded view.

Cockpit seat

Cockpit sole

TOP VIEW

Centre division

Intermediate division

Bearer

Runner fixed to seat side

Lip stop

Rope flakes down into rope box

12

300

Drawbolts

Gap for drainage

Drain holes

Cockpit sole

FRONT VIEW

SECTIONAL SIDE VIEW

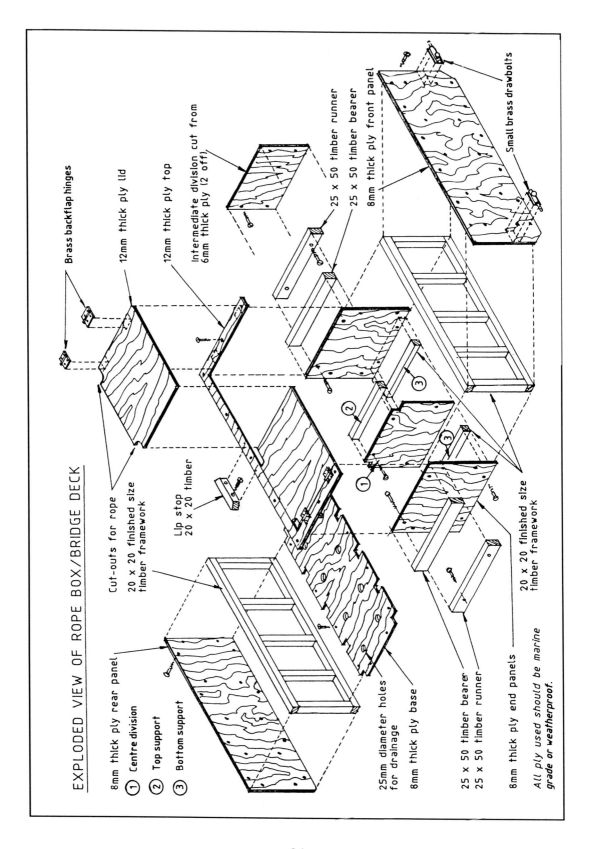

EXPLODED VIEW OF ROPE BOX/BRIDGE DECK

8mm thick ply rear panel

① Centre division

② Top support

③ Bottom support

Brass backflap hinges

12mm thick ply lid

12mm thick ply top

Intermediate division cut from
6mm thick ply (2 off)

25 x 50 timber runner

25 x 50 timber bearer

8mm thick ply front panel

Small brass drawbolts

Cut-outs for rope

20 x 20 finished size
timber framework

Lip stop
20 x 20 timber

25mm diameter holes
for drainage

8mm thick ply base

25 x 50 timber bearer

25 x 50 timber runner

8mm thick ply end panels

20 x 20 finished size
timber framework

All ply used should be marine
grade or weatherproof.

Rope Box/Bridge Deck

Materials required

1 × length Timber, 25 mm × 50 mm × 1600 mm
Timber for framework, 20 mm × 20 mm, length to suit vessel
12 mm Marine or Weatherproof Plywood, amount to suit vessel
8 mm Marine or Weatherproof Plywood, amount to suit vessel
6 mm Marine or Weatherproof Plywood, amount to suit vessel
4 × Brass Backflap Hinges, 30 mm wide
24 × No 6 Brass Countersunk Screws, 9 mm long
6 × No 8 Brass Countersunk Screws, 30 mm long
4 × No 6 Brass Countersunk Screws, 18 mm long
9 × No 8 Brass Countersunk Screws, 25 mm long
8 × No 4 Brass Countersunk Screws, 8 mm long
2 × small Brass Drawbolts

Construction

Measure the distance between the cockpit seats. This will be the overall length of the rope box less 6 mm for clearance. Determine the depth and height and cut out end panels in 8 mm plywood. Cut 25 × 50 mm timber bearers and screw fix these to end panels. Cut 20 × 20 mm timber and make the front and rear frames. Cut front and rear panels and fix to the frames. Fix end panels to the frames. Cut 20 × 20 mm timber bottom supports and screw to the end panels. Cut and make the base from 8 mm ply. Cut out the drain holes and fix it in position.

Next, cut the division panels and fix the top support to the centre division. Fix the top panel and lids, including the cut-outs for rope insertion. Care is needed to ensure that the lids when lifted will clear the lip stop and any other obstructions on the bulkhead.

Place the rope box in position between the seat sides. Next, cut and fix the runners in position; these screw fix to the seat sides to support the rope box. When slid into position these runners are masked by the front panels of the box. Cut and fix the lip stop in position; this screws to the bulkhead to stop the box lifting in rough weather. Finally, fix the hinges and drawbolts and paint or varnish to complete.

Rope Box/
Bridge Deck

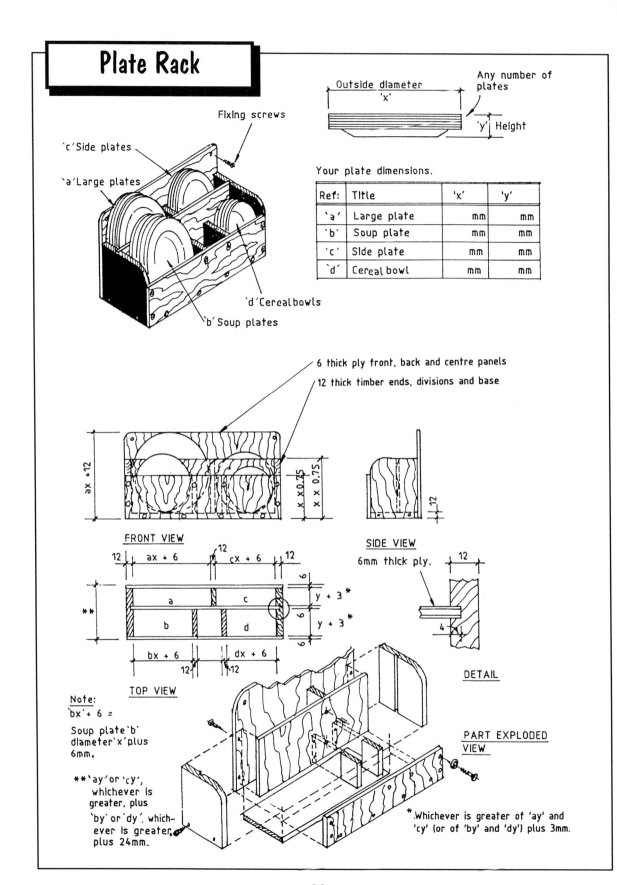

Plate Rack

Materials required

6 mm Marine or Weatherproof Plywood, for size see sketch
10 × No 8 Brass Countersunk Screws, 25 mm long
26 × No 6 Brass Countersunk Screws, 18 mm long
12 × No 6 Brass Screw Cups
2 × No 6 Brass Fixing Screws

Construction

Carefully measure the outside plate diameter (x) and the stack height (y), and insert these figures in the appropriate boxes on the sketch. Divide your plates into two groups according to dimension 'y', in other words thin plates and deeper bowls. Whichever has the greater 'y' dimension will dictate the breadth of the divisions.

Taking the 6 mm thick ply and starting from a right-angled corner mark out the rear panel as shown on the sketch. The outside width will be the plate diameter plus 6 mm for clearance. The rear panel height will be the diameter of the largest plate plus 12 mm. Cut out the rear panel.

Mark out the middle and front panels as shown. Please note that the middle panel will be 16 mm narrower than the front and rear panels (see detail on sketch). The middle panel height will be three-quarters of the diameter of the smaller of the rear plates. The front panel will be three-quarters of the

diameter of the smaller of the front plates.

Using the 12 mm thick timber, cut out the end pieces and the divisions and also the base (note the base fits inside the end pieces). Drill the middle panel first and fix the timber divisions using the 18 mm No 6 screws. Mark the position of the middle panel on the end pieces and cut the grooves to suit the middle ply panel; these should be a tight fit. Shape and round the front top corners of the ends and screw them to the base using the 25 mm No 8 screws. Slot the middle panel in position and screw the base to the centre divisions from underneath. Screw on the front and rear panels, using the brass screw cups on the front face only.

Clean up with glasspaper. Round the corners and drill two holes for fixing the unit to a bulkhead or partition. Varnish or paint as desired.

A Plate Rack

Under-Deckhead Plate Rack

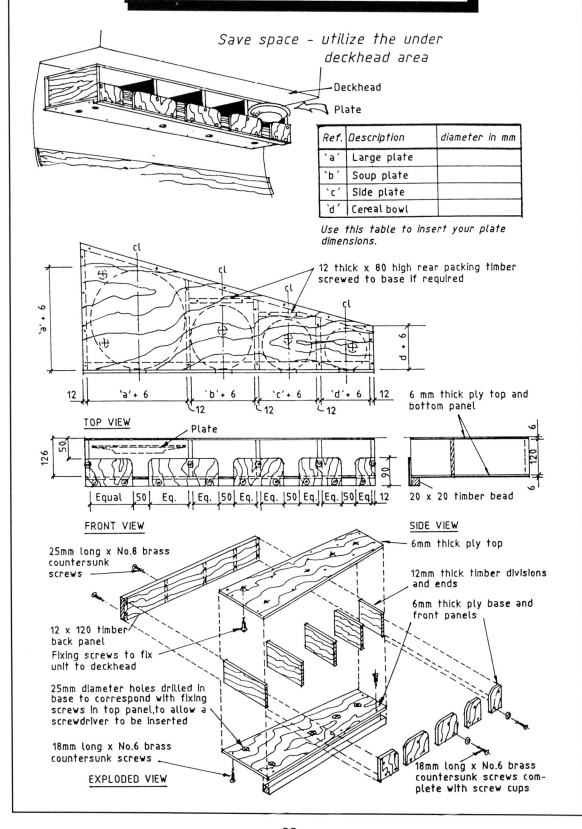

Save space - utilize the under deckhead area

Deckhead

Plate

Ref.	Description	diameter in mm
'a'	Large plate	
'b'	Soup plate	
'c'	Side plate	
'd'	Cereal bowl	

Use this table to insert your plate dimensions.

12 thick x 80 high rear packing timber screwed to base if required

TOP VIEW

6 mm thick ply top and bottom panel

Plate

FRONT VIEW

SIDE VIEW

20 x 20 timber bead

6mm thick ply top

25mm long x No.8 brass countersunk screws

12mm thick timber divisions and ends

6mm thick ply base and front panels

12 x 120 timber back panel

Fixing screws to fix unit to deckhead

25mm diameter holes drilled in base to correspond with fixing screws in top panel, to allow a screwdriver to be inserted

18mm long x No.6 brass countersunk screws

EXPLODED VIEW

18mm long x No.6 brass countersunk screws complete with screw cups

Under-Deckhead Plate Rack

Materials required

6 mm Marine or Weatherproof Plywood, for size see sketch
Timber, 12 mm × 80 mm, for length see sketch
Timber, 12 mm × 126 mm, for length see sketch
44 × No 6 Brass Countersunk Screws, 18 mm long
14 × No 6 Brass Screw Cups
10 × No 8 Brass Countersunk Screws, 25 mm long
4 × Screws or Bolts to fix unit to deckhead
1 × Timber Bead, 20 mm × 20 mm, for length see sketch

Construction

It is advisable to obtain your plates first as they vary in size. Carefully measure their overall diameters and write these figures in the boxes on the sketch.

Mark out the top panel on the 6 mm thick ply. Starting at a right-angled corner, allow 12 mm for the end panel then mark off the diameter of the largest plate plus 6 mm. Continue through to the smallest plate, allowing for the 12 mm thick divisions between the plates.

Mark the centreline (d) of each plate and measure off from the front the diameters of the smallest and largest plates plus 6 mm for clearance. Draw a diagonal line to intersect these two points. A further 12 mm outside this first line, draw another parallel line. This will give you the outside size and shape of the top panel. Make sure that all your plates will fit into their allotted space. If any of the plates foul the first line, then the panel must be widened to accommodate them. Cut out the top panel and a corresponding bottom panel.

Next, out of the 126 mm wide timber cut the back to the correct length (the angle can be trimmed after construction) and screw in position to the bottom panel. From the same timber cut out the divisions and end pieces and screw in position to the bottom panel. Cut the 20 mm × 20 mm timber bead to length and fix this to the underside of the bottom panel, along the front edge only.

Check that the plates fit easily between the divisions. In order to stop the middle plates sliding too far back in their respective compartments it may be necessary to fit packing timber behind the plates at the rear. If this is required it should be fixed before the top panel is screwed in position. Screw the top panel to the unit. On the front edge mark the centreline position of each plate on to the 20 mm × 20 mm bead and make a small mark 25 mm each side of this line. This will indicate the gap positions. Cut 6 mm ply to make the front pieces. Drill and screw in position as shown on the sketch using the brass screw cups. Check that the plates will pass over the top of these panels and stack neatly behind.

Determine both the method and positions for fixing the unit to the underside of the deckhead. These will differ from boat to boat depending on the construction. If the unit is to be screwed up under the deckhead, mark the positions on the top panel and drill to suit the bolts or screws that you will use. Exactly beneath these positions drill a 25 mm diameter hole in the bottom panel. This will enable a screwdriver to be inserted from below to tighten the screws.

Clean up the unit with glasspaper and varnish or paint as desired. Finally, screw or bolt the unit into its final position.

Cockpit-Mounted Echo-Sounder Bracket

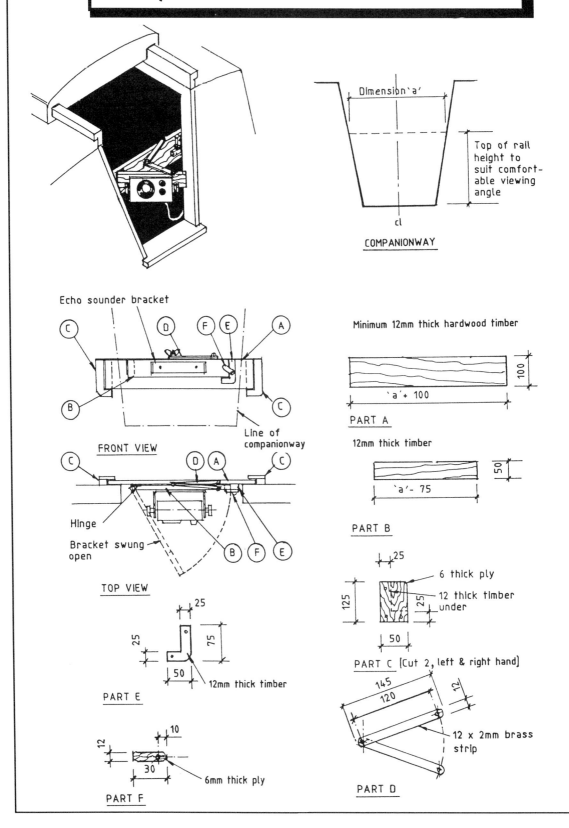

Dimension 'a'

Top of rail height to suit comfortable viewing angle

cl

COMPANIONWAY

Echo sounder bracket

FRONT VIEW

Line of companionway

TOP VIEW

Hinge

Bracket swung open

Minimum 12mm thick hardwood timber

100

'a' + 100

PART A

12mm thick timber

50

'a' – 75

PART B

25

6 thick ply

12 thick timber under

125

25

50

PART C (Cut 2, left & right hand)

145

120

12

12 x 2mm brass strip

PART D

25

75

25

50

12mm thick timber

PART E

10

12

30

6mm thick ply

PART F

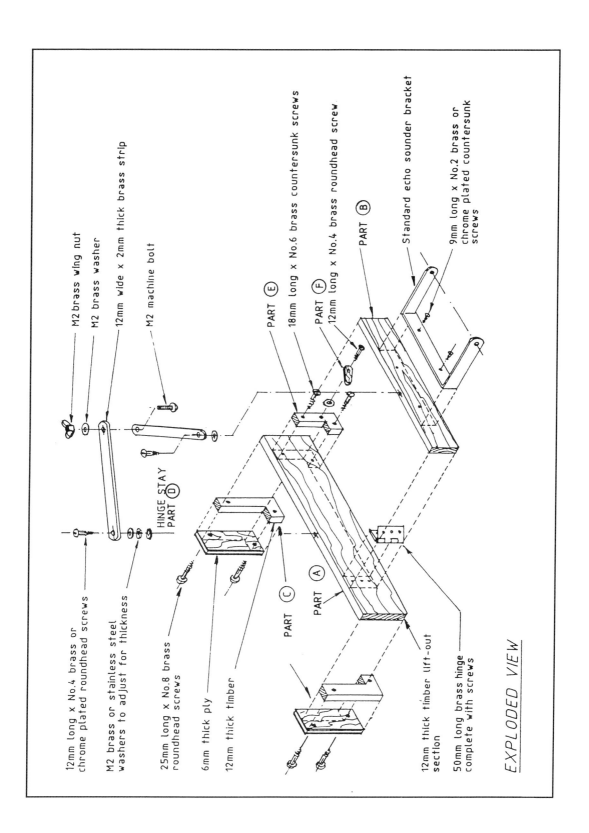

M2 brass wing nut

M2 brass washer

12mm wide x 2mm thick brass strip

M2 machine bolt

PART (E)

18mm long x No.6 brass countersunk screws

PART (F)

12mm long x No.4 brass roundhead screw

PART (B)

Standard echo sounder bracket

9mm long x No.2 brass or chrome plated countersunk screws

12mm long x No.4 brass or chrome plated roundhead screws

M2 brass or stainless steel washers to adjust for thickness

25mm long x No.8 brass roundhead screws

6mm thick ply

12mm thick timber

HINGE STAY PART (D)

PART (C)

PART (A)

12mm thick timber lift-out section

50mm long brass hinge complete with screws

EXPLODED VIEW

41

Cockpit-Mounted Echo-Sounder Bracket

How many times, when sailing short-handed, has there been no one to go below to call out the depth to the helmsman? The answer is simple: bring the echo-sounder within sight of the helmsman. There are two versions, lift-out and fold-away, most of the parts for which are the same.

Materials required

Hardwood, 12 mm × 100 mm (finished size), length to suit companionway
Hardwood, 12 mm × 50 mm (finished size), length to suit companionway
Hardwood for parts 'C' and 'E', 12 mm × 50 mm (finished size) × 400 mm
6 mm Marine or Weatherproof Plywood for parts 'C' and 'F', approximately 130 mm × 130 mm
2 × Brass Flat Strips, 2 mm × 12 mm × 150 mm
1 × M2 Brass Machine Bolt, with Wing Nut and Washer
6 × M2 Brass Washers
2 × No 2 Brass or Chrome Countersunk Screws, 9 mm long
3 × No 4 Brass or Chrome Roundhead Screws, 12 mm long
4 × No 8 Brass Roundhead Screws, 25 mm long
2 × No 6 Brass Countersunk Screws, 18 mm long
1 × Brass Hinge, 50 mm long, with Brass Countersunk Screws, 12 mm long

Construction (lift-out version)

First decide at what height in the companionway you need to mount the echo-sounder. At this height measure the width of the opening. This is dimension 'a'.

Cut the 100 mm wide × 12 mm thick timber to the length of dimension 'a' plus 100 mm (part 'A' in sketch).

Next cut out two L-shaped pieces from the 400 mm long × 50 mm wide timber (part 'C'). Cut two pieces of ply 125 mm × 50 mm and screw-fix these over the L-shaped pieces, so that they finish handed left and right. Fix these on the inside of the companionway, so that part 'A' will slot into them. Part 'A' should be sanded so that it slides in easily.

Cut the 50 mm wide timber to the length of dimension 'a' less 75 mm (part 'B'). Fix 'A' to 'B' with the hinge and with the top faces of the timber in line. Cut out and make parts 'E' and 'F' and fix in position as shown on drawing.

Cut, drill and shape the 12 mm wide × 2 mm thick brass strip to form the hinge stays (part 'D'). These screw onto the top faces of timbers 'A' and

'B' and can be fixed either way round, but for the greatest opening angle the fixing screws should be closer to the hinge end. It is a better arrangement to braze the hinge bolt to the bottom stay arm, but if this is not possible it will still perform satisfactorily. Finally, smooth with glasspaper, round any sharp edges, and varnish or paint as preferred.

An inside storage position can be arranged in any convenient location within the boat by duplicating part 'C'. The whole arrangement (parts 'A', 'B', 'D', 'E' and 'F') can simply be lifted out from part 'C' and slotted into the brackets inside. Make sure that the electrical connection cable is long enough to reach both positions.

Construction (fold-away version)

The construction of a fold-away bracket instead of a lift-out version will require a clear area into which the bracket can be folded back. This version will not require parts 'C', but will require two additional parts 'E' and 'F' and an additional brass hinge and screws. Part 'A' may need to be lengthened to suit the second hinge position.

When folded back out of the way or when in position the end opposite to the hinge will need supporting by the addition of two part 'E' and 'F' assemblies, one fixed to the inside of the companionway replacing part 'C' and one to support the unhinged end when folded back. The rest of the construction is the same for the fold-away version as it is for the lift-out version.

A Cockpit-Mounted Echo-Sounder Bracket

Clothes Drier

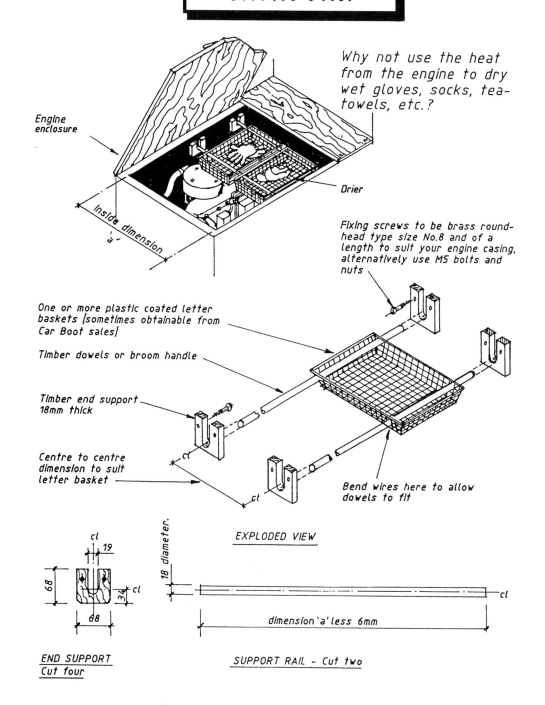

Why not use the heat from the engine to dry wet gloves, socks, tea-towels, etc.?

Engine enclosure

Inside dimension 'a'

Drier

Fixing screws to be brass round-head type size No.8 and of a length to suit your engine casing, alternatively use M5 bolts and nuts

One or more plastic coated letter baskets (sometimes obtainable from Car Boot sales)

Timber dowels or broom handle

Timber end support 18mm thick

Centre to centre dimension to suit letter basket

Bend wires here to allow dowels to fit

cl

19

68

34

68

cl

cl

18 diameter.

EXPLODED VIEW

cl

dimension 'a' less 6mm

END SUPPORT
Cut four

SUPPORT RAIL - Cut two

The baskets complete with the support rails can be quickly and easily removed should the need arise to get at the engine. Ensure that the completed installation does not impede any function of the engine.

Clothes Drier

Materials required

2 × 18 mm diameter Timber Dowels, for length see sketch
4 × pieces Timber or Marine or Weatherproof Plywood, 18 mm × 68 mm × 68 mm
8 × No 8 Brass Roundhead Screws or M5 Bolts and Nuts, length to suit engine casing
2 × Plastic-Coated Wire Letter Trays/Baskets

Construction

Measure the inside width of your engine compartment. This will be dimension 'a'. Cut two 18 mm diameter dowels (or broom handles) to length (dimension 'a' less 6 mm).

Cut out the four end supports as shown on the sketch, and ensure that the dowels will fit easily into the slots. Drill the end supports for screw or bolt fixings. Thread the letter tray(s) onto the dowels and slot into position. The wires on the baskets can be manipulated slightly to accommodate the dowels.

Making sure that the basket is clear of the engine and will not impede any engine function, mark the position of the centrelines of the dowels on the inside of the engine casing. Fix the end supports in position and make sure the dowels slot in easily.

A Clothes Drier

Bow Roller

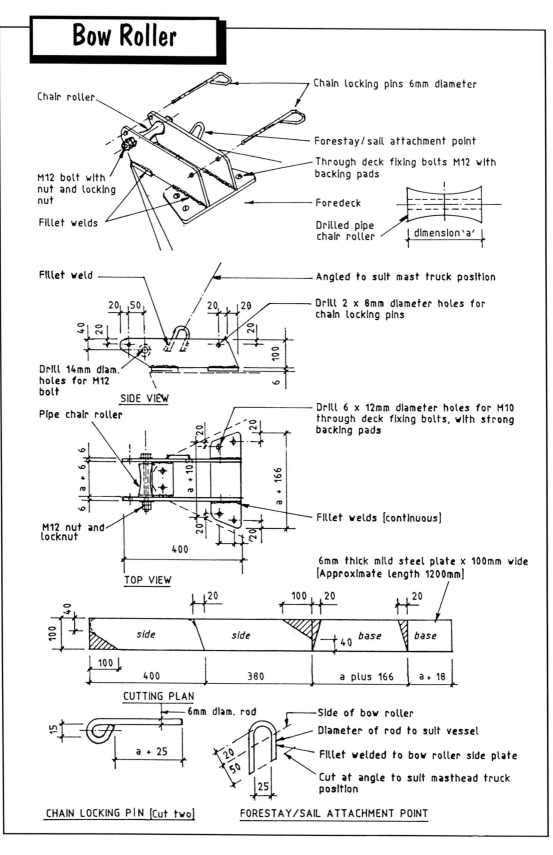

Chain locking pins 6mm diameter

Chair roller

Forestay/sail attachment point

Through deck fixing bolts M12 with backing pads

M12 bolt with nut and locking nut

Foredeck

Fillet welds

Drilled pipe chair roller

dimension 'a'

Fillet weld

Angled to suit mast truck position

Drill 2 x 8mm diameter holes for chain locking pins

20 | 50 | 20 | 20

40 | 20

100

Drill 14mm diam. holes for M12 bolt

6

SIDE VIEW

Pipe chair roller

Drill 6 x 12mm diameter holes for M10 through deck fixing bolts, with strong backing pads

6 + 6

20 | 20

a + 6

a + 10

a + 166

6

Fillet welds [continuous]

M12 nut and locknut

20 | 20

400

TOP VIEW

6mm thick mild steel plate x 100mm wide [Approximate length 1200mm]

40

100

20 | 100 | 20 | 20

side | side | base | base

40

100

400 | 380 | a plus 166 | a + 18

CUTTING PLAN

6mm diam. rod

Side of bow roller

15

Diameter of rod to suit vessel

a + 25

20

50

Fillet welded to bow roller side plate

Cut at angle to suit masthead truck position

25

CHAIN LOCKING PIN [Cut two]

FORESTAY/SAIL ATTACHMENT POINT

Bow Roller

To make a bow roller you will need access to a welder and you will also need to obtain a pipe chair roller about 4 inches (100 mm) long. This latter item may be obtained from a heating engineering firm.

Materials required

1 × Pipe Chair Roller
1 × piece 6 mm Mild Steel Plate, 100 mm × 1200 mm
2 × lengths 6 mm diameter Mild Steel Rod, 250 mm long
1 × length Mild Steel Rod, diameter to suit forestay terminal, 200 mm long
1 × M12 Hexagon Bolt, length dimension 'a' + 58 mm, with Nut, Locking Nut and Washers
6 × M10 Stainless Steel, Galvanised or Painted Mild Steel Hexagon Fixing Bolts, length to suit deck thickness, with Nuts and Washers

Construction

First measure the length of your pipe chair roller, this will become your dimension 'a'. Next mark and cut out your mild steel plate as shown in the sketch; dimensions can be modified to suit your deck layout. Weld the various parts together as shown using fillet type welds. Then drill the various holes as shown on the sketch. Bolt the chair roller in position using plenty of washers and ensure that the roller turns easily. Next, using the 6 mm diameter rod make the two chain locking pins.

Remove the foredeck forestay fitting if it is in the way of the bow roller position. Mark the position and weld the forestay attachment point to the bow roller. Take special care with the welding as all the parts need to be very strong to take the high loads that they will be subjected to. Alternatively, the bow roller can be fitted to one side of the forestay, in which case you will not need to fit the forestay attachment point.

Clean up and paint with *Galvafroid*, Zinc or *Hammerite* paint. Alternatively, the whole thing can be galvanised or made from stainless steel.

Finally, drill through the deck and, using a backing plate or oversized washers, bolt the bow roller into position. Apply a suitable mastic before tightening bolts.

A Bow Roller

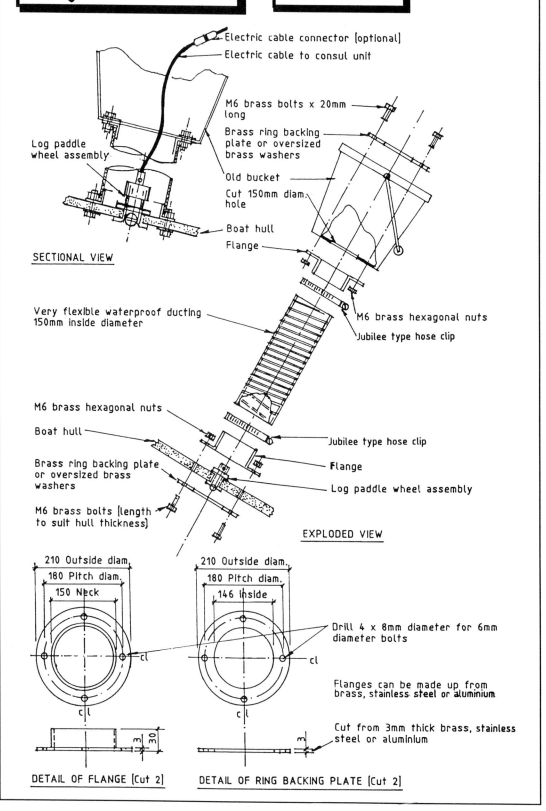

Electric cable connector (optional)

Electric cable to consul unit

M6 brass bolts x 20mm long

Brass ring backing plate or oversized brass washers

Old bucket

Cut 150mm diam. hole

Log paddle wheel assembly

Boat hull

Flange

SECTIONAL VIEW

Very flexible waterproof ducting 150mm inside diameter

M6 brass hexagonal nuts

Jubilee type hose clip

M6 brass hexagonal nuts

Boat hull

Brass ring backing plate or oversized brass washers

M6 brass bolts (length to suit hull thickness)

Jubilee type hose clip

Flange

Log paddle wheel assembly

EXPLODED VIEW

210 Outside diam.

180 Pitch diam.

150 Neck

cl

cl

DETAIL OF FLANGE (Cut 2)

210 Outside diam.

180 Pitch diam.

146 inside

cl

cl

DETAIL OF RING BACKING PLATE (Cut 2)

Drill 4 x 8mm diameter for 6mm diameter bolts

Flanges can be made up from brass, stainless steel or aluminium

Cut from 3mm thick brass, stainless steel or aluminium

Log Paddle Wheel – removal aid

Materials required

1 × length 150 mm diameter Very Flexible Waterproof Duct or Hose, length to suit vessel's draught (i.e. paddle wheel to waterline plus 150 mm)
2 × Angle Flanges to suit internal diameter of duct or hose. These can be made up from brass, stainless steel or aluminium
2 × 150 mm diameter Jubilee Hose Clips
1 × Plastic or Rubber Bucket
2 × Brass Backing Rings or Oversize Washers
4 × M6 Brass or Stainless Steel Fixing Bolts, 20 mm long, with Nuts and Washers
4 × M6 Brass or Stainless Steel Through-Hull Fixing Bolts, length to suit hull thickness, with Nuts and Washers

Something I get quite worried about is the removal of the log paddle wheel, whether for cleaning or replacement whilst at sea. Unscrewing the fitting and removing the paddle wheel assembly from the inside, leaving an open hole in the bottom of the boat of 25 mm or so, fills me with alarm. What if I can't screw it back again or I drop the vital part into the bilges, never to be found again?

The log paddle wheel removal aid gives one some confidence. The arrangement shown in the sketch enables the safe removal of the wheel assembly. By tying the bucket up as high as possible, you won't have to rush the job, providing of course that the top of the bucket is well above the waterline. To replace the paddle wheel simply push your hand inside the bucket and down the flexible tube, and screw back the assembly. Then remove the small amount of water that has collected in the tube.

This arrangement can either be installed permanently or made removable. If removable, you will need to be able to disconnect the electric cable. This will require a cable connector. Check with your log/paddle wheel manufacturer to ensure that the installation of this connector will not adversely affect the function of your log.

Construction

Cut a 150 mm diameter hole in the bucket and fix one of the flanges as shown on the sketch using the 20 mm long bolts and the backing ring or washers. Ensure a good mastic seal around the joints.

Position the other flange in the bottom of the vessel centrally around the paddle wheel assembly. Drill holes for the fixing bolts through the hull and backing ring or oversized washer. Fit bolts washers and nuts, and tighten. Ensure a good mastic seal around all joints. Slip the flexible duct over the flanges and secure with the hose clips.

If fitting a removable aid you must be able to disconnect the cable connection. To remove, simply disconnect the cable, undo the lower hose clip and slide off.

Note

A suitable type of ducting is *Flexflyte U8* silicone-coated flexible duct, manufactured by Flexible Ducting Ltd., Cloberfield, Milngavie, Glasgow, Scotland, G62 7LW

Life belt Holder

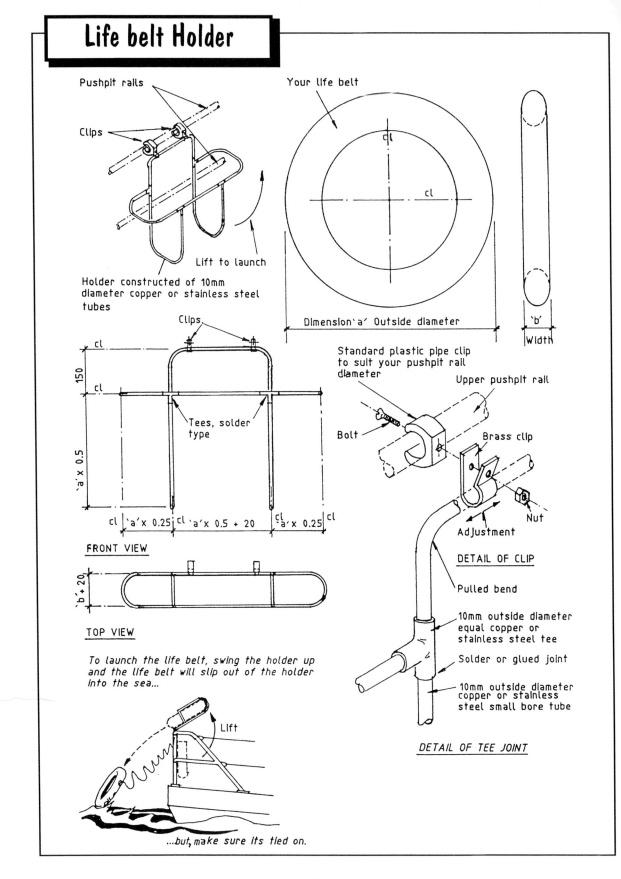

Pushpit rails

Clips

Your life belt

Holder constructed of 10mm diameter copper or stainless steel tubes

Lift to launch

Dimension 'a' Outside diameter

'b' Width

cl

Clips

150

cl

cl

Tees, solder type

'a' x 0.5

cl 'a' x 0.25 cl 'a' x 0.5 + 20 cl 'a' x 0.25 cl

FRONT VIEW

'b' + 20

TOP VIEW

To launch the life belt, swing the holder up and the life belt will slip out of the holder into the sea...

Lift

...but, make sure its tied on.

Standard plastic pipe clip to suit your pushpit rail diameter

Upper pushpit rail

Bolt

Brass clip

Nut

Adjustment

DETAIL OF CLIP

Pulled bend

10mm outside diameter equal copper or stainless steel tee

Solder or glued joint

10mm outside diameter copper or stainless steel small bore tube

DETAIL OF TEE JOINT

Life Belt Holder

Materials required

1 × length 10 mm outside diameter Microbore Copper or Stainless Steel Tube, length dimension 'a' × 6
4 × 10 mm equal Copper Capillary Tees (pre-soldered) or Stainless Steel Tees (adhesive type)
2 × Plastic Pipe Clips (as shown in sketch), to suit outside diameter of pushpit rail
2 × Brass Strips, 2 mm × 10 mm × 50 mm
2 × Brass or Stainless Steel Countersunk Bolts, diameter and length (approximately 30 mm) to suit plastic clips, with Nuts

Construction

First measure the outside diameter and the width of your life belt. These are dimensions 'a' and 'b'. Bend and cut the two lower pipe supports and carefully trim to the same length. Next, bend and cut the rear support pipe and finally the two side pipes and the front member. All the dimensions on the sketch are taken from pipe centrelines, so when cutting allow for the socket connection of the tees.

Assemble the holder dry and check that the life belt slips in and out easily. Make sure each pipe is pushed fully home at the tee.

If using copper tube, clean the ends of the tubes where they connect to the tees with wire wool and apply a skin of flux. As we are not looking for a water tight joint, it is not necessary to clean the inside of the tees. Then apply heat with a blowlamp evenly over each tee until the solder starts to flow. Heat the three joints of each tee together. Stop applying heat as soon as the solder runs. Overheating will only allow the solder to run out of the joint leaving none inside to effect the bond.

If using stainless steel tube, use epoxy resin or the manufacturer's adhesive and glue the fittings in place. Manufacturer's adhesives are like super glue; *do not touch with the fingers*.

Clean up the holder. From the two brass strips, fashion the small clips and drill a hole through both lugs to suit the pipe clip. Using the nuts and bolts, fix the bracket/clip assembly together, locking the top support pipe in the brass clips. Clip the holder to the inside of the top rail of your pushpit.

Note

Bending copper pipes is not too difficult and with care you should be able to form nice rounded bends, but don't try and make them too sharp or the pipe will kink. Bending stainless steel pipes, however, is much more difficult and I would suggest that you try to borrow a microbore bender from your local plumber, or make one (see 'Mini Tube Bender').

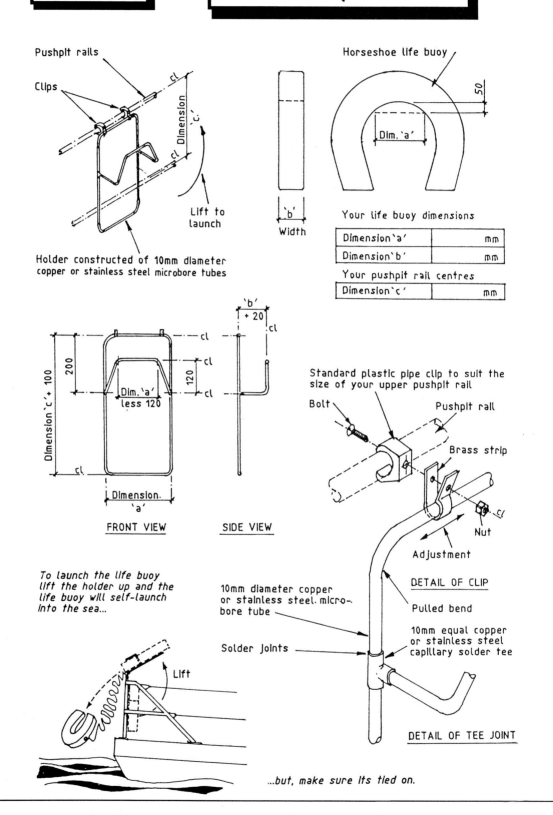

Pushpit rails

Clips

Dimension 'c'

Lift to launch

Holder constructed of 10mm diameter copper or stainless steel microbore tubes

Horseshoe life buoy

50

Dim. 'a'

'b'

Width

Your life buoy dimensions

Dimension 'a'	mm
Dimension 'b'	mm

Your pushpit rail centres

Dimension 'c'	mm

Dimension 'c' + 100

200

120

Dim. 'a' less 120

Dimension 'a'

FRONT VIEW

'b' + 20

SIDE VIEW

Standard plastic pipe clip to suit the size of your upper pushpit rail

Bolt

Pushpit rail

Brass strip

Nut

Adjustment

DETAIL OF CLIP

Pulled bend

10mm diameter copper or stainless steel microbore tube

10mm equal copper or stainless steel capillary solder tee

Solder joints

DETAIL OF TEE JOINT

To launch the life buoy lift the holder up and the life buoy will self-launch into the sea...

Lift

...but, make sure its tied on.

52

Horseshoe Life Buoy Holder

Materials required

1 × length 10 mm outside diameter Microbore Copper or Stainless Steel Tube,
length (dimension 'c' × 2) + (dimension 'a' × 3) + 800 mm
2 × 10 mm equal Copper Capillary Tees (pre-soldered) or Stainless Steel Tees (adhesive type)
2 × Plastic Pipe Clips (as shown in sketch), to suit outside diameter of pushpit rail
2 × Brass Strips, 2 mm × 10 mm × 50 mm
2 × Brass or Stainless Steel Countersunk Bolts, diameter and length to suit plastic clips, with Nuts

Construction

First measure the three dimensions 'a', 'b' and 'c' as shown and enter these dimensions on the sketch. Note that all dimensions on the holder are from centreline to centreline. Cut and bend the three pieces of tube to form the holder as shown. Trim the lengths of the three parts so that the ends are level. Clean the ends of all the copper tubes with wire wool and make sure they fit into the tees.

With the holder assembled dry, check that the life buoy will slip over the front 'hook' section. It can be bent out or in to facilitate this.

If using copper tube, flux the ends of each of the pipes and assemble into the tees. Apply heat evenly over each tee until the solder starts to flow. Heat the three joints of each tee together. If using stainless steel tube, then assemble using adhesive (or as per manufacturer's recommendations). Keep adhesives away from the skin.

To complete the holder see previous instructions for 'Life Belt Holder'.

Mini-Tube Bender

Tube

Pulley wheel

Calibration marks

Pin 'A'

Pin 'B'

Handle

To obtain dimension 'a'

Pulley wheel

Tube

Bolt

cl

cl

cl

'a'

Tube feed

Pulley wheel

44

25

180°

200

25

22

300

90°

135°

22

cl 'a' cl

60

190

10

Pin 'A'

TOP VIEW

cl

3

Pull to bend.

SIDE VIEW-Pin 'A'

Pulley wheel

Locknut

Nut

Nut

Nut

Bolt

cl

M6 bolt

Locknut

Washers

3

Dimension 'a'

SIDE VIEW-Pin 'B'

8mm thick ply

22 x 44 finished size
softwood timber

Pin 'B'

cl

15

a

cl

400

25

DETAIL OF HANDLE

Locknut

Nut

M6 bolt

Washers

Handle

Nuts

No.8 brass
countersunk
wood screws

Nuts

Washers

180°

135°

30°

M6 bolt

Large bolt [see
text]

EXPLODED VIEW

54

Mini-Tube Bender

Materials required

1 × 8 mm Plywood Offcut, approximately 200 mm × 300 mm
2 × pieces Softwood, 22 mm × 44 mm (finished size) × 200 mm
1 × small Engine Pulley Wheel with groove to suit tube (see sketch). Pulley wheels can be obtained from car-breakers or engine spare parts suppliers etc.
2 × M6 Hexagonal Bolts, with Nuts
1 × Bolt, diameter to suit hole in pulley wheel, length pulley wheel thickness + 50 mm, with 4 Nuts and selection of Washers
4 × No 8 Brass Countersunk Wood Screws, 19 mm long
1 × length Mild Steel Flat Bar, 3 mm × 25 mm × 400 mm

Construction

Fix the softwood support timbers to the ply base using the four wood screws. Place the pulley wheel on the centreline of the base, to one side as shown on the sketch. Drill a hole in the base the same size as the hole in the pulley and bolt the wheel temporarily in position. Place a short length of tube in the groove of the pulley wheel and position one of the bolts (pin 'A') against it, as in the sketch (top right). This gives you the centreline of the bolt, but drill the actual hole for it 10 mm nearer to the rear of the base (see top view).

Cut and round the corners of the flat bar to form the handle, and drill two holes in it the same sizes and distance apart as the holes in the base.

You are now ready to assemble the bender. Push the large bolt up through the base and secure it in place by tightening down the first nut. Next, put on one or more washers and then the pulley itself, securing it with the second nut. The wheel does not have to turn, although it does not matter if it does. On top of one or more further washers fit the handle with another washer on top, followed by a nut and locking nut. The handle should be loose enough to move freely, but tight enough not to sag.

Now cut the two M6 bolts (pins 'A' and 'B') to length as shown in side views, allowing sufficient clearance. Fit the bolts with their nuts to the base and handle respectively.

Operation

Turn the handle anticlockwise until the two pins come together. Slide the tube between the groove of the pulley wheel and the pins, until sufficient length is protruding to form the bend. Holding the pipe and the base down firmly with one hand, move the handle clockwise until the required angle of bend is achieved. Return the handle anticlockwise to release the pipe. Marks can be scored on the base under the leading edge of the handle to correspond with different degrees of bend.

Pulled bends look so much neater than the results of trying to bend pipes over your knee or by hand and this simple arrangement can produce quite professional looking results. Persevere – practice makes perfect.

Recessed Engine Controls

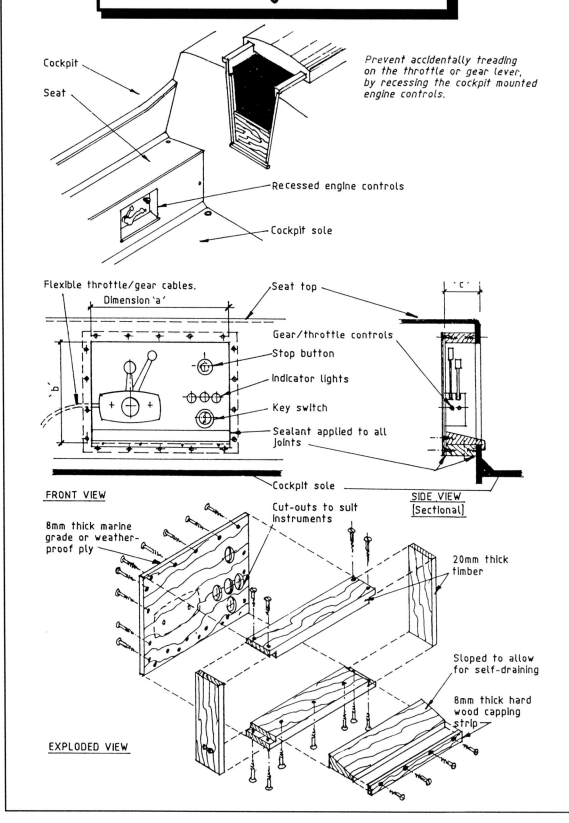

Cockpit

Seat

Prevent accidentally treading on the throttle or gear lever, by recessing the cockpit mounted engine controls.

Recessed engine controls

Cockpit sole

Flexible throttle/gear cables.

Dimension 'a'

Seat top

'c'

Gear/throttle controls

Stop button

Indicator lights

Key switch

Sealant applied to all joints

Cockpit sole

FRONT VIEW

SIDE VIEW
[Sectional]

Cut-outs to suit instruments

8mm thick marine grade or weather-proof ply

20mm thick timber

Sloped to allow for self-draining

8mm thick hard wood capping strip

EXPLODED VIEW

Recessed Engine Controls

Materials required

1 × piece 8 mm Marine or Weatherproof Plywood, (dimension 'a' + 40 mm) × (dimension 'b' + 40 mm)
1 × piece Timber, 20 mm × dimension 'c', length 2 × ('a' + 'b') + 160 mm
1 × piece Timber tapered to self-drain (see sketch), 50 mm × dimension 'c' × dimension 'a'
1 × Hardwood Strip, 8 mm × 25 mm × dimension 'a'
40 × No 6 Brass Countersunk Wood Screws, 18 mm long
8 × No 8 Brass Countersunk Wood Screws, 25 mm long
3 × No 8 Brass Countersunk Wood Screws, 32 mm long

If you have an auxiliary yacht, how many times has a crew member jumped back into the cockpit, caught the engine control lever with their foot and either knocked the engine out of gear or suddenly increased the revs, or even gone sprawling across the cockpit? Anything that sticks out on a vessel can be a safety hazard. This arrangement enables you to recess the cockpit engine controls and minimize any mishaps.

Dimensions 'a', 'b' and 'c' will depend on your cockpit arrangement, length and travel of gear lever, throttle lever etc. Most cockpit engine controls work with push-pull cables and are easily moved without much work. Make your recess big enough to allow room for your hands to operate the controls.

Construction

First disconnect the throttle, gear lever and stop button from their cables and remove these items. If you have any other controls (e.g. a key switch or indicator lights) these will also need to be disconnected and removed. Mark out the aperture ('a' × 'b') on the cockpit side, but make sure that you have enough room on the inside to accommodate the recess and further room for installing the gear and throttle mechanisms. With a jigsaw or coping saw cut out the aperture.

Cut the 20 mm thick timber into four lengths to line the aperture. Each piece will need to be approximately 40 mm longer or higher than the aperture. Using half butt joints (see sketch) form a frame to line the aperture, the inside face of the frame being flush with the edge of the aperture.

Use the eight 25 mm long screws to screw the frame together. Use waterproof glue on all the joints.

Next, drill the fixing holes around the aperture approximately 10 mm in from the edge. Using the 18 mm long screws fix the frame to the inside of the aperture. Use a waterproof glue or suitable sealant to make a watertight joint.

Cut the 8 mm thick ply to form the back panel. Drill and fix with 18 mm long screws. Shape the tapered timber, cut to length and fix from underneath with the three 32 mm long screws. Again, all joints should be made watertight. Cut the 8 mm thick hardwood strip to length. Drill and fix with waterproof glue and 18 mm long screws.

All that now remains is to cut the necessary holes in the back panel and re-fix all the controls in the recess. Sand all the woodwork and varnish or paint. If your cockpit sides are of GRP construction then you may prefer to fibre-glass the recess before attaching the controls. If this is the case you will not require the hardwood capping strip. Make sure when making a fibre-glass joint that the cloth is overlapped by at least 50 mm.

Fairleads

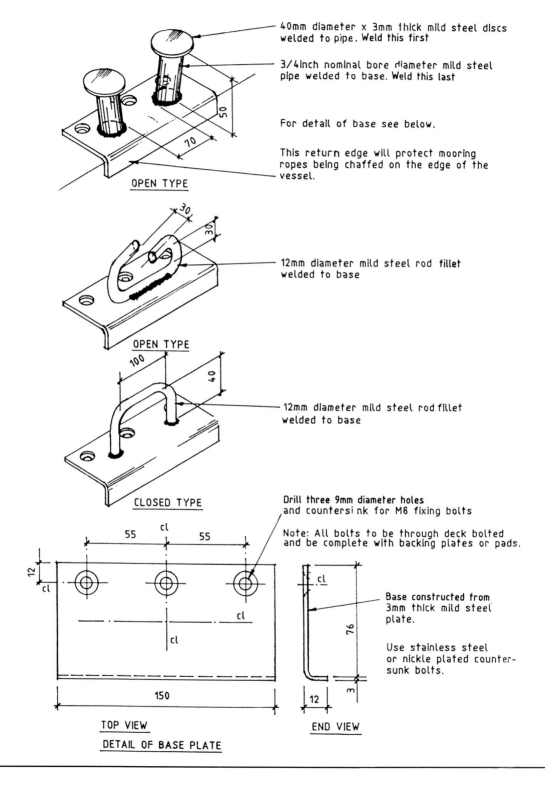

40mm diameter x 3mm thick mild steel discs welded to pipe. Weld this first

3/4inch nominal bore diameter mild steel pipe welded to base. Weld this last

For detail of base see below.

This return edge will protect mooring ropes being chaffed on the edge of the vessel.

OPEN TYPE

12mm diameter mild steel rod fillet welded to base

OPEN TYPE

12mm diameter mild steel rod fillet welded to base

CLOSED TYPE

Drill three 9mm diameter holes and countersink for M8 fixing bolts

Note: All bolts to be through deck bolted and be complete with backing plates or pads.

Base constructed from 3mm thick mild steel plate.

Use stainless steel or nickle plated counter-sunk bolts.

TOP VIEW

END VIEW

DETAIL OF BASE PLATE

Fairleads

Ventilator Protectors

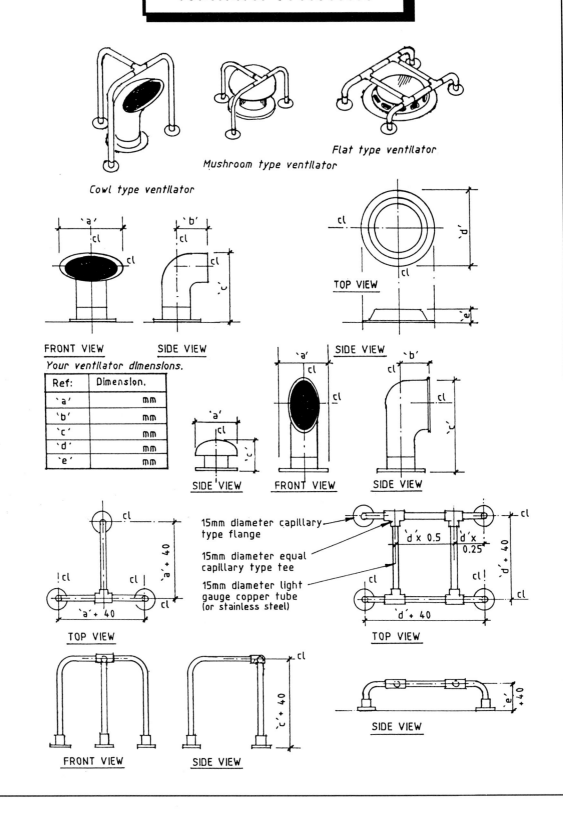

Cowl type ventilator

Mushroom type ventilator

Flat type ventilator

FRONT VIEW

SIDE VIEW

TOP VIEW

SIDE VIEW

Your ventilator dimensions.

Ref:	Dimension.	
'a'		mm
'b'		mm
'c'		mm
'd'		mm
'e'		mm

SIDE VIEW

FRONT VIEW

SIDE VIEW

TOP VIEW

15mm diameter capillary type flange

15mm diameter equal capillary type tee

15mm diameter light gauge copper tube (or stainless steel)

'd' x 0.5   'd' x 0.25

TOP VIEW

FRONT VIEW

SIDE VIEW

SIDE VIEW

Ventilator Protectors

Materials required

For cowl type:
1 × length 15 mm outside diameter Light-Gauge Copper or Light-Gauge Stainless Steel Tube, length (dimension 'a' × 2) + (dimension 'c' × 3) + 200 mm
1 × 15 mm equal Copper Capillary Tee (pre-soldered) (Yorkshire Fitting Catalogue No YP24 or similar) or Stainless Steel Tee (adhesive type)
3 × 15 mm Copper Capillary Flange Connector or Floor Plate (pre-soldered) (Yorkshire Fitting Catalogue No YP112 or YP112A or similar) or Stainless Steel Fitting (adhesive type)
Screws or Bolts to fix flanges or floor plates to deck or coachroof

For flat type:
1 × length 15 mm outside diameter Light-Gauge Copper or Stainless Steel Tube, length (dimension 'd' × 4) + (dimension 'e' × 4) + 240 mm
4 × 15 mm equal Copper or Stainless Steel Tees (as for cowl type)
4 × 15 mm Copper Flange Connector or Floor Plate or Stainless Steel Fitting (as for cowl type)
Screws or Bolts to fix flanges or floor plates to deck or coachroof

Plastic ventilators are considerably cheaper than their metal counterparts but have one serious drawback: they are susceptible to damage on the deck or coachroof where they are usually fixed. These simple ventilator protectors can be made easily from either light-gauge copper tubes using capillary solder fittings or light-gauge stainless steel tubes and adhesive fittings. The pulled bends shown in the sketch can be replaced with elbows or pre-formed bends if preferred.

There are three main types of ventilator, which are shown in the sketch. The protector for the 'mushroom' type is basically the same as that for the cowl type.

Construction

Enter the dimensions of your particular ventilator in the boxes contained in the sketch.

If pulling the bends, do this first before cutting the tubes to length. With copper tube a bending spring can be used to form the bends, obtainable from any ironmonger or plumbing shop. The spring should be greased with 'tallow' and a thin rope attached to one end. The spring is put inside the tube and it can then be bent over the knee to the required angle. Then, by pulling the rope the coils are stretched enabling the spring to be pulled out of the tube.

Stainless steel tubes are much stronger than copper and you will require access to a bending machine. These can sometimes be hired from a plant hire firm and are easy to use. Alternatively you could use ready-made elbows or bends instead, but this will involve additional joints to be either soldered or stuck with adhesive. None of the joints need to be watertight.

Cut the tubes to the required lengths and assemble the pieces dry first. If using soldered fittings, thoroughly clean the ends of all the tubes with wire wool and coat with flux. Assemble once more and, using a blow lamp, apply heat to each fitting evenly until the ring of solder contained in it runs out of the joint. Do not overheat; once the solder has filled the joint, that is enough. Always heat all the joints of any fitting together. If using adhesive fittings follow manufacturer's instructions for assembling the joints.

Clean off all joints when cold and paint if desired. Screw fix or through-bolt in position over the ventilator.

Opening Portlight

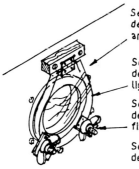

See assembly 'A' for details of external flange and ring.

See assembly 'B' for details of inside portlight.

See assembly 'C' for details of lugs and fixing clips.

See assembly 'D' for details of hold-back.

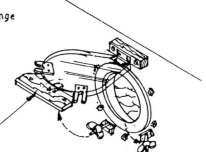

PORTHOLE CLOSED

PORTHOLE OPEN

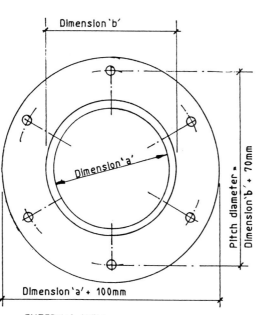

Dimension 'b'

Dimension 'a'

Pitch diameter = Dimension 'b' + 70mm

Dimension 'a' + 100mm

EXTERNAL VIEW

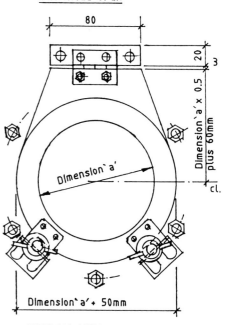

80

20

3

Dimension 'a' x 0.5 plus 60mm

cl.

Dimension 'a'

Dimension 'a' + 50mm

INTERNAL VIEW

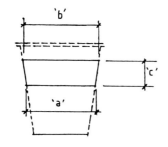

'b'

'c'

'a'

Cut section from your plastic flowerpot

Dimensions		
Ref.	Description	Size
a	Internal portlight diameter	mm
b	External portlight diameter	mm
c	Thickness of yacht hull	mm

Thickness of perspex/polycarbonate.		
River	Minimum thickness	6mm
Coastal	Minimum thickness	8mm
Ocean	Minimum thickness	12mm

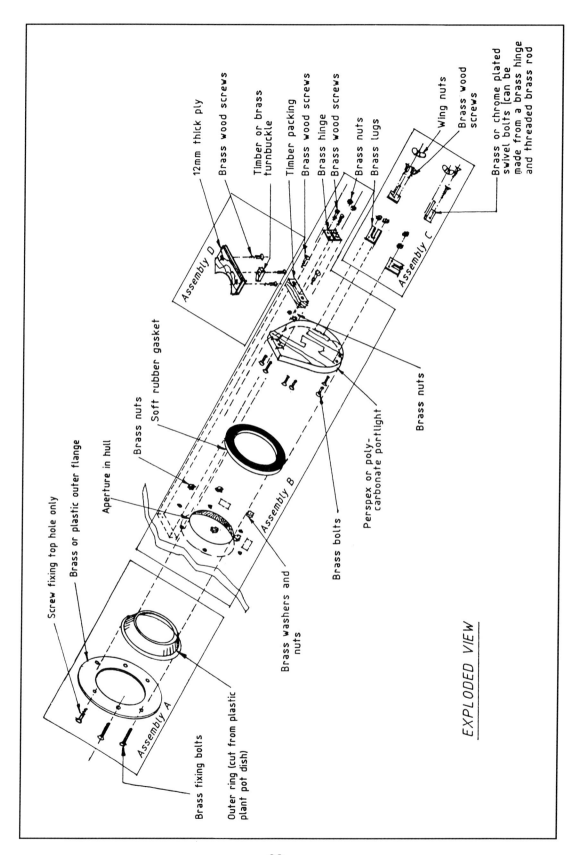

Screw fixing top hole only

Brass or plastic outer flange

Aperture in hull

Brass nuts

Soft rubber gasket

12mm thick ply

Brass wood screws

Timber or brass turnbuckle

Timber packing

Brass wood screws

Brass hinge

Brass wood screws

Brass nuts

Brass lugs

Wing nuts

Brass wood screws

Brass or chrome plated swivel bolts [can be made from a brass hinge and threaded brass rod

Assembly D

Assembly C

Brass nuts

Perspex or poly-carbonate portlight

Brass bolts

Assembly B

Brass washers and nuts

Outer ring (cut from plastic plant pot dish)

Brass fixing bolts

Assembly A

EXPLODED VIEW

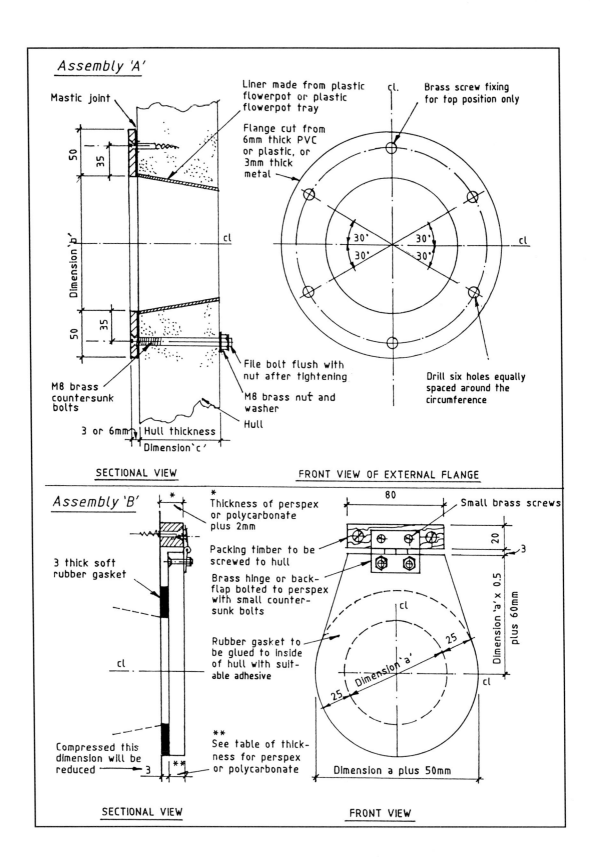

Assembly 'A'

Mastic joint

Liner made from plastic flowerpot or plastic flowerpot tray

Flange cut from 6mm thick PVC or plastic, or 3mm thick metal

Brass screw fixing for top position only

cl.

50

35

Dimension 'b'

cl

50

35

30° 30°

30° 30°

cl

M8 brass countersunk bolts

File bolt flush with nut after tightening

M8 brass nut and washer

Hull

Drill six holes equally spaced around the circumference

3 or 6mm Hull thickness

Dimension 'c'

SECTIONAL VIEW

FRONT VIEW OF EXTERNAL FLANGE

Assembly 'B'

*

* Thickness of perspex or polycarbonate plus 2mm

Packing timber to be screwed to hull

Brass hinge or back-flap bolted to perspex with small counter-sunk bolts

Rubber gasket to be glued to inside of hull with suitable adhesive

80

Small brass screws

20

3

3 thick soft rubber gasket

Dimension 'a' x 0.5 plus 60mm

cl

cl

25

Dimension 'a'

25

cl

Compressed this dimension will be reduced

3

**

** See table of thickness for perspex or polycarbonate

Dimension a plus 50mm

SECTIONAL VIEW

FRONT VIEW

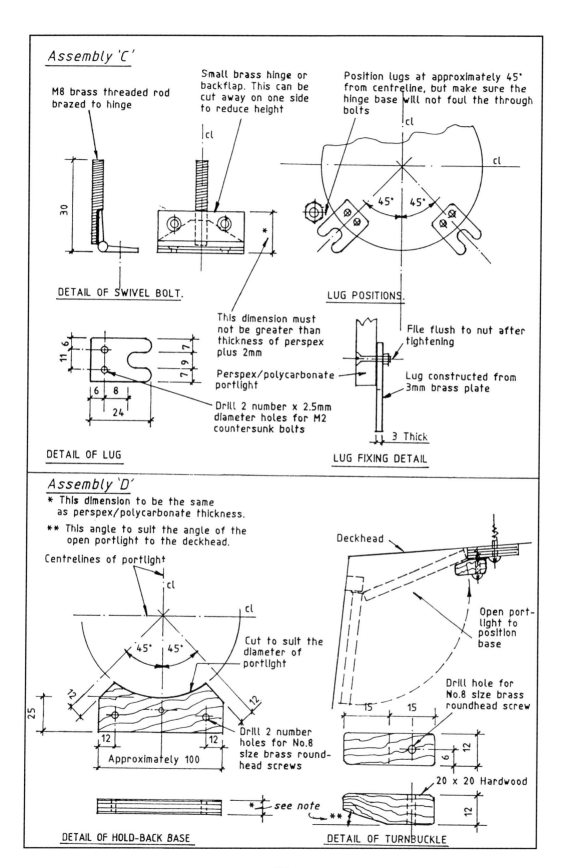

Assembly 'C'

M8 brass threaded rod brazed to hinge

Small brass hinge or backflap. This can be cut away on one side to reduce height

Position lugs at approximately 45° from centreline, but make sure the hinge base will not foul the through bolts

DETAIL OF SWIVEL BOLT.

LUG POSITIONS.

This dimension must not be greater than thickness of perspex plus 2mm

File flush to nut after tightening

Perspex/polycarbonate portlight

Lug constructed from 3mm brass plate

Drill 2 number x 2.5mm diameter holes for M2 countersunk bolts

3 Thick

DETAIL OF LUG

LUG FIXING DETAIL

Assembly 'D'

* This dimension to be the same as perspex/polycarbonate thickness.

** This angle to suit the angle of the open portlight to the deckhead.

Centrelines of portlight

Deckhead

Cut to suit the diameter of portlight

Open port-light to position base

Drill hole for No.8 size brass roundhead screw

Drill 2 number holes for No.8 size brass round-head screws

Approximately 100

20 x 20 Hardwood

* see note

**

DETAIL OF HOLD-BACK BASE

DETAIL OF TURNBUCKLE

65

Opening Portlight

Opening portlights can be a very expensive item to purchase, especially if you have a large vessel. This arrangement endeavours to provide a cheap but strong home-made alternative.

Materials required

1 × Plastic Flower Pot or Flower Pot Tray, base diameter dimension 'a' (i.e. the size of porthole you require)
1 × piece Clear Perspex or Polycarbonate Sheet, for thickness see table, (dimension 'a' + 50 mm) × (dimension 'a' + 85 mm)
1 × piece 6 mm PVC or Plastic Sheet, diameter dimension 'a' + 100 mm
1 × piece 3 mm Soft Rubber, diameter dimension 'a' + 50 mm
1 × piece Timber for packing, 20 mm × 20 mm × 80 mm
1 × small Brass Butt or Backflap Hinge, approximately 40 mm long
1 × piece Plywood, thickness to suit perspex or polycarbonate sheet, approximately 40 mm × 100 mm
1 × piece Hardwood, 12 mm × 12 mm (finished size) × 30 mm
2 × small Butt or Backflap Hinges
1 × M8 Brass Threaded Rod, 60 mm long
2 × Brass Strips, 3 mm thick, approximately 24 mm × 24 mm
Brass Screws, Bolts, Nuts and Washers to suit vessel

Construction

Most of the dimensions of your portlight will depend upon the size of the plastic flower pot or flower pot tray that you select. The reason a flower pot is used as a liner is that, because of its tapered sides, any water will self-drain away from the seal and back into the sea. With thin hulls it may be possible to do away with the liner altogether, though it is a good idea to retain the flanged outer ring as a reinforcement to the hull.

Having selected your plastic flower pot, measure the thickness of your hull and cut and form the liner as shown for assembly 'A'. After cutting the aperture in the hull, fix the liner. This can be secured in place with a good quality mastic sealant (*Sikaflex* or similar). Next, cut and shape the external ring flange. Drill it for the bolts and fix into place with mastic. The top fixing should be screwed rather than through-bolted, but can be bolted by reversing the countersunk bolt so that there is no possibility of the nut fouling the inside hinge arrangement.

Now cut out the rubber gasket and the perspex (see assembly 'B'). Stick the gasket to the inside of the hull using a suitable adhesive.

Trim the timber packing piece so that when the perspex is pressed against the gasket the timber is slightly thinner than it. This is necessary as when the wing nuts are tightened on the swivel bolts the rubber is compressed making a good seal. If the timber is too thick you will not achieve this. Screw the packing piece in position.

Next, fix the hinge in position. The top half is screwed to the packing piece and the lower half is through-bolted to the perspex window, all as shown in assembly 'B'.

You now need to attach the lugs and the swivel or hinged bolts. You can, of course, buy swivel or hinged bolts, but they are quite expensive. I have therefore shown a method of making these, using brass threaded rod and hinges, provided you have the facility to braze the two together. If you have to have these brazed by an engineering firm, then it will probably be cheaper to buy your swivel bolts from the chandler.

If you prefer the challenge, however, first cut and trim the half of the hinge which will carry the threaded rod so that it does not stand higher than the thickness of the perspex plus 2 mm. Cut the threaded brass rod to the desired length and carefully file a flat on one side (see assembly 'C') to accommodate the hinge. The two parts can now be brazed together.

Then cut and shape the two lugs out of the brass strip. Drill and fix them to the perspex with countersunk bolts, the heads of which should be on the side facing the gasket. The brazed swivel bolts can now be positioned and the hinge bolted or screwed to the hull. Wing nuts complete the construction and when slackened should permit the bolts to be folded down to allow the perspex window to be lifted.

The portlight can be held in the open position by a simple bungee cord retainer, or if you prefer you can use a 'hold-back' as shown in assembly 'D'. This hold-back screw-fixes or bolts to the deckhead and has a small hardwood turnbuckle to secure, shaped as shown in assembly 'D'. If the perspex opens parallel to the deckhead, then a brass turnbuckle or a 2p cupboard clip may be used instead.

The hold-back base is cut from an offcut of ply and should be shaped to accommodate the curve of the perspex and be short enough to miss the brass lugs. It may be necessary to have the ply thicker than the perspex to allow for the lugs. Alternatively, the base can be tapered to be parallel with the opened portlight.

Note

When drilling perspex for bolts, always ensure that the bolts fit loosely to avoid cracking the perspex.

Toilet Seat Hold-Back

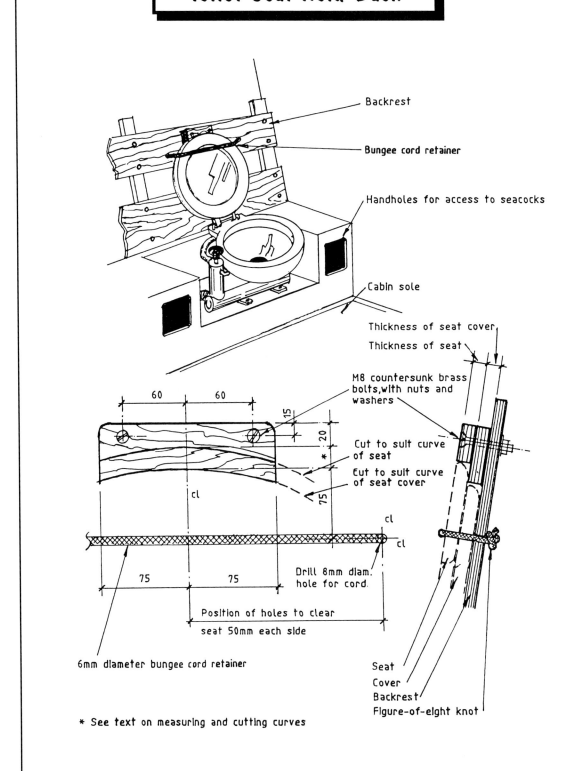

Backrest

Bungee cord retainer

Handholes for access to seacocks

Cabin sole

Thickness of seat cover

Thickness of seat

M8 countersunk brass bolts, with nuts and washers

Cut to suit curve of seat

Cut to suit curve of seat cover

60   60

15

20

*

75

cl

cl

cl

Drill 8mm diam. hole for cord.

75   75

Position of holes to clear seat 50mm each side

6mm diameter bungee cord retainer

Seat
Cover
Backrest
Figure-of-eight knot

* See text on measuring and cutting curves

Toilet Seat Hold-Back

Materials required

2 × pieces Plywood, thickness to suit toilet seat and lid, 60 mm × 150 mm
2 × M8 Brass Countersunk Bolts, approximately 35 mm long, with Nuts and Washers
1 × length 6 mm Bungee or Shock Cord, approximately 760 mm long

Construction

Lift the seat of the toilet and mark on the backrest the position of the vertical centreline and top of the seat.

Clamp the two pieces of plywood together and drill the two holes for the countersunk bolts. Holding the two pieces together, place in position against the backrest so that the vertical centreline is in line with the centreline on the backrest and the mark for the top of the seat is 20 mm below the top of the ply.

Holding or clamping them in this position, drill the holes for the bolts right through the backrest or, if there is no backrest, screw the ply to the wall or bulkhead.

Lift the lid and the seat and with a pencil scribe the curve of the top of the seat on the top piece of ply. Unbolt and remove the top piece and re-bolt or screw the bottom piece only in position. Lift the lid and scribe the curve on this piece. Remove the ply and cut out the curves using a jigsaw or a coping saw. Finally, sand smooth. When re-assembled the lid and the seat should both fit snugly against the ply.

To fit the bungee cord, drill an 8 mm hole in the backrest on either side of the seat in the raised position, about 75 mm below the top and 50 mm out from the side. Smooth those holes well with glasspaper. Thread the bungee and tie a figure-of-eight knot at each end.

If you do not have a backrest, then you will need two small lacing eyes with screws to fit the bungee cord.

Cheap Rubbing Strake

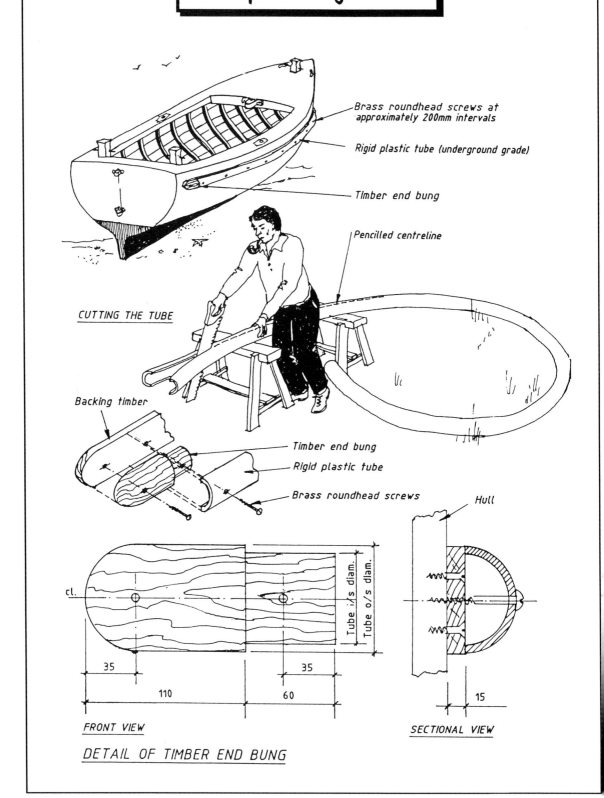

Brass roundhead screws at approximately 200mm intervals

Rigid plastic tube (underground grade)

Timber end bung

Pencilled centreline

CUTTING THE TUBE

Backing timber

Timber end bung

Rigid plastic tube

Brass roundhead screws

Hull

Tube i/s diam.

Tube o/s diam.

cl.

35

110

35

60

15

FRONT VIEW

SECTIONAL VIEW

DETAIL OF TIMBER END BUNG

70

Cheap Rubbing Strake

Materials required

1 × length Rigid Plastic Tube, diameter and length to suit your vessel. Use heavy grade tube, as for underground gas or water mains, colour-coded yellow or blue
4 × pieces Hardwood, half outside diameter of tube × outside diameter of tube × 170 mm
2 × lengths Timber, 15 mm × outside diameter of tube × length of rubbing strake required
Brass Countersunk Screws for backing timber
Brass Roundhead Screws for tube

Construction

After cutting the tube to length mark a centreline along the whole length, keeping the tube as straight as possible. Then cut the tube lengthways into two equal halves using a panel saw or a jigsaw.

From the hardwood construct and shape the end bungs as described on the sketch so that they fit snugly into the ends of the half tubes.

Cut the timber backing pieces and fix to the hull, after rounding the ends to match the end bungs. The backing pieces are fixed to the hull with countersunk brass screws or bolts.

Next screw-fix the half tubes to the backing pieces using the roundheaded screws. Mastic should be applied to the edges of the tube before fixing to prevent the ingress of water.

Finally, fit the end bungs into position and fix with roundheaded screws. The inner screw secures the tube to the end bung. End bungs should be fitted to both ends of the tube. They can be sanded and varnished to provide an attractive finish.

Rubbing strakes can be reinforced by sheathing with fibreglass matt and resin. In some cases the rubbing strake can be fixed direct to the hull without the use of the timber backing strips.

Spray Hood

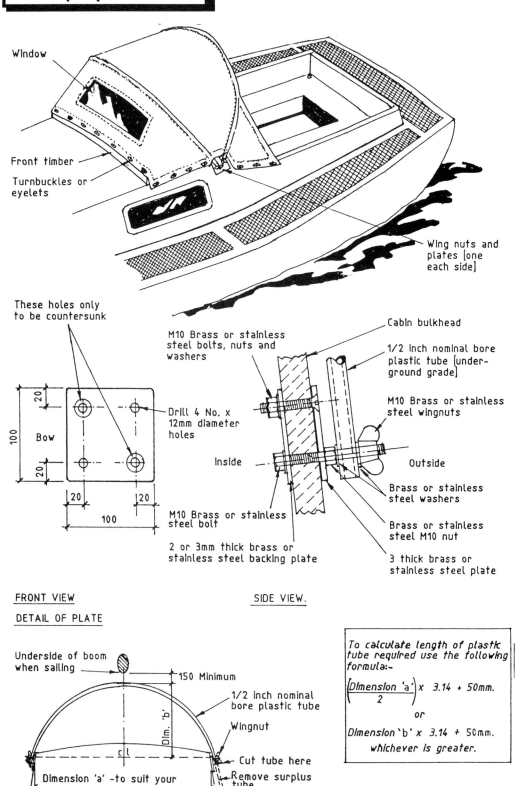

Window

Front timber

Turnbuckles or eyelets

Wing nuts and plates (one each side)

These holes only to be countersunk

M10 Brass or stainless steel bolts, nuts and washers

Cabin bulkhead

1/2 inch nominal bore plastic tube (underground grade)

M10 Brass or stainless steel wingnuts

20

100

Bow

20

20   20

100

Drill 4 No. x 12mm diameter holes

Inside

Outside

Brass or stainless steel washers

Brass or stainless steel M10 nut

M10 Brass or stainless steel bolt

2 or 3mm thick brass or stainless steel backing plate

3 thick brass or stainless steel plate

FRONT VIEW

DETAIL OF PLATE

SIDE VIEW.

Underside of boom when sailing

150 Minimum

1/2 inch nominal bore plastic tube

Wingnut

Dim. 'b'

c l

Cut tube here

Remove surplus tube

Dimension 'a' -to suit your cabin top

To calculate length of plastic tube required use the following formula:-

$$\left(\frac{\text{Dimension 'a'}}{2}\right) \times 3.14 + 50mm.$$

or

Dimension 'b' x 3.14 + 50mm.

whichever is greater.

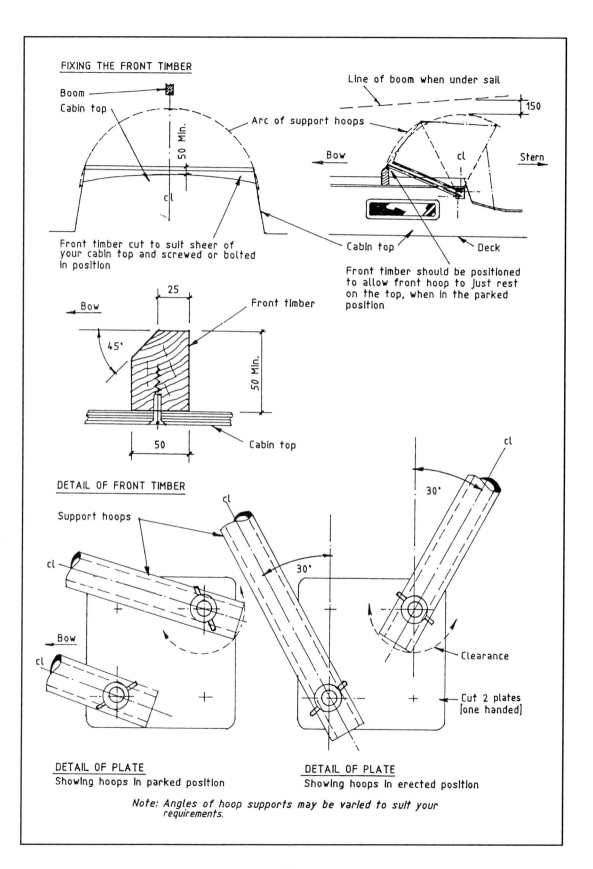

FIXING THE FRONT TIMBER

Boom
Cabin top

50 Min.

cl

Front timber cut to suit sheer of
your cabin top and screwed or bolted
in position

Line of boom when under sail

150

Arc of support hoops

Bow   cl   Stern

Cabin top   Deck

Front timber should be positioned
to allow front hoop to just rest
on the top, when in the parked
position

Bow

25

45°

Front timber

50 Min.

50

Cabin top

DETAIL OF FRONT TIMBER

Support hoops

cl

cl   30°

Bow   cl

cl

30°

Clearance

Cut 2 plates
(one handed)

DETAIL OF PLATE
Showing hoops in parked position

DETAIL OF PLATE
Showing hoops in erected position

Note: Angles of hoop supports may be varied to suit your
requirements.

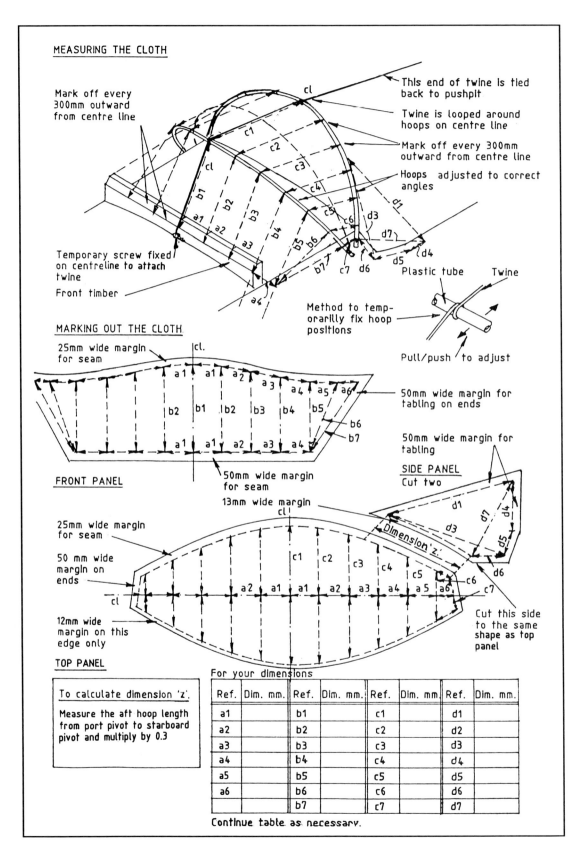

MEASURING THE CLOTH

Mark off every 300mm outward from centre line

This end of twine is tied back to pushpit

Twine is looped around hoops on centre line

Mark off every 300mm outward from centre line

Hoops adjusted to correct angles

Temporary screw fixed on centreline to attach twine

Front timber

Method to temporarilly fix hoop positions

Plastic tube   Twine

Pull/push to adjust

MARKING OUT THE CLOTH

25mm wide margin for seam

50mm wide margin for tabling on ends

50mm wide margin for tabling

SIDE PANEL
Cut two

FRONT PANEL

50mm wide margin for seam

13mm wide margin

25mm wide margin for seam

50 mm wide margin on ends

12mm wide margin on this edge only

Cut this side to the same shape as top panel

Dimension 'z'.

TOP PANEL

To calculate dimension 'z'.

Measure the aft hoop length from port pivot to starboard pivot and multiply by 0.3

For your dimensions

Ref.	Dim. mm.	Ref.	Dim. mm.	Ref.	Dim. mm.	Ref.	Dim. mm.
a1		b1		c1		d1	
a2		b2		c2		d2	
a3		b3		c3		d3	
a4		b4		c4		d4	
a5		b5		c5		d5	
a6		b6		c6		d6	
		b7		c7		d7	

Continue table as necessary.

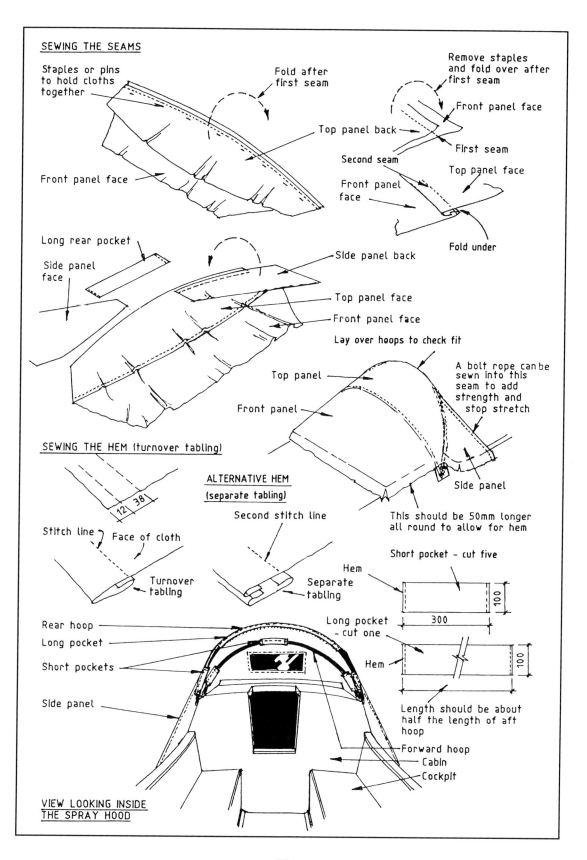

SEWING THE SEAMS

Staples or pins to hold cloths together

Fold after first seam

Front panel face

Remove staples and fold over after first seam

Front panel face

Top panel back

First seam

Second seam

Top panel face

Front panel face

Fold under

Long rear pocket

Side panel face

Side panel back

Top panel face

Front panel face

Lay over hoops to check fit

Top panel

Front panel

A bolt rope can be sewn into this seam to add strength and stop stretch

SEWING THE HEM (turnover tabling)

12 38

Stitch line   Face of cloth

Turnover tabling

ALTERNATIVE HEM
(separate tabling)

Second stitch line

Separate tabling

Side panel

This should be 50mm longer all round to allow for hem

Short pocket - cut five

Hem

300

100

Long pocket - cut one

Hem

100

Length should be about half the length of aft hoop

Rear hoop

Long pocket

Short pockets

Side panel

Forward hoop

Cabin

Cockpit

VIEW LOOKING INSIDE
THE SPRAY HOOD

75

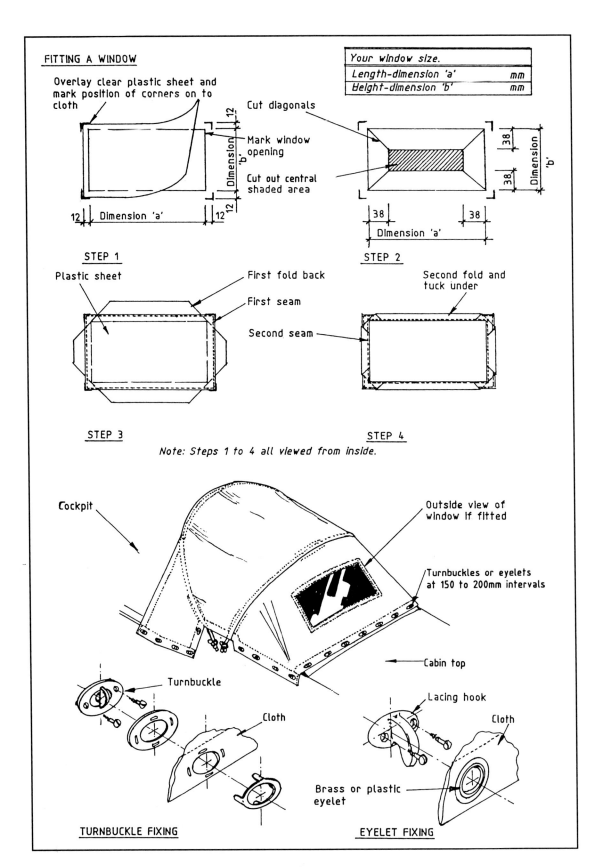

FITTING A WINDOW

Overlay clear plastic sheet and mark position of corners on to cloth

Cut diagonals

Mark window opening

Cut out central shaded area

Your window size.	
Length-dimension 'a'	mm
Height-dimension 'b'	mm

Dimension 'b'

Dimension 'a'

12

12

38

38

Dimension 'a'

Dimension 'b'

STEP 1

STEP 2

Plastic sheet

First fold back

First seam

Second fold and tuck under

Second seam

STEP 3

STEP 4

Note: Steps 1 to 4 all viewed from inside.

Cockpit

Outside view of window if fitted

Turnbuckles or eyelets at 150 to 200mm intervals

Cabin top

Turnbuckle

Cloth

Lacing hook

Cloth

Brass or plastic eyelet

TURNBUCKLE FIXING

EYELET FIXING

76

Spray Hood

Now if you like something a bit more challenging why not make yourself a spray hood.

Materials required

2 × Brass or Stainless Steel Plates, 3 mm × 100 mm × 100 mm
2 × Brass or Stainless Steel Plates, 2 mm or 3 mm × 100 mm × 100 mm
4 × M10 Brass or Stainless Steel Countersunk Bolts, length to suit your cabin sides + 18 mm
4 × M10 Brass or Stainless Steel Hexagon Bolts, length to suit your cabin sides + 60 mm
2 × lengths ½ inch nominal bore Heavy Gauge Plastic Tube for support hoops, for length see sketch. Tube should be semi-rigid, as for underground gas or water mains.
4 × M10 Brass or Stainless Steel Nuts
4 × M10 Brass or Stainless Steel Wing Nuts
16 × M10 Brass or Stainless Steel Washers
1 × length Hardwood, 50 mm × depth of cabin top camber + 50 mm × length of width of cabin top
Canvas or Sailcloth, approximately one-and-a-half times the width of your cabin top square (e.g. if your cabin top is 2 metres wide you will require 9 square metres)
Clear Plastic Sheet for window, size as desired (obtainable from camping tent suppliers)
Turnbuckles and Screws or Eyelets, Lacing Hooks and Screws as preferred

Making hinge plates and hoops

First decide where your hinge plates will have to go. This requires some forward thinking. Try to imagine the hoops assembled and visualize where they will be in both the upright and parked positions. Avoid any obstructions, like ventilators, although control line cleats and the companionway can usually be accommodated within the arc of the hoops when parked. The front timber may have to be modified to allow control lines to pass through, either by purpose-made slots or holes. Cabin top handholds may need to be cut back or enclosed.

Construct your hinge plates. If using stainless steel, then the backing plates, nuts and bolts should also be of stainless steel or alternatively the whole can be made with brass plates and nuts and bolts. It is generally not a good idea to mix dissimilar metals as this can cause electrolytic corrosion in salt water.

Of the four fixing holes in each plate, two will be used for fixing only and two through-bolted to leave a length of thread on the outside which will be the pivots for your support hoops. Through-bolting avoids having to braze or weld threaded rod to the plates.

Next, take the plastic tube. It usually curls slightly as it is supplied in large coils. Drill a 12 mm diameter hole 25 mm in from one end, and fix in position on one of the pivots, securing with the washers and wing nut. Curve the tube over the cabin top to the other side and adjust to the required height. Drill a second hole to line up with the bolt on that side. Slip it over the pivot and secure with a wing nut. Cut off any surplus tube an inch (25 mm) from the centre of the hole. The height must not impede the movement of the boom when under sail, for obvious reasons, and I would suggest that a minimum clearance of 150 mm is allowed.

Repeat the exercise with the second plastic tube. Your hoop frames are now complete.

To fit the front timber, its position on the cabin top must first be determined. Ideally it should be positioned so that when the hoops are laid down flat the top part of the curve rests across the timber. It can be moved further towards or away from the hinge position if desired. Having marked the position on the cabin top, the timber must now be shaped to suit the camber at that point. When this has been done, the ends should be cut to the width of the cabin top and sloped if necessary to suit the angle of the sides of the cabin. Finally a bevel must be formed on the forward edge of the timber (see sketch for details). If you have sheets and halyards led back to the cockpit via the cabin top, a slot or cutout must be made to allow their free passage. Be sure to round and smooth all edges well to avoid chafe on these ropes.

The front timber may now be treated and varnished (or painted) and fixed down to the cabin top with mastic sealant and suitable brass screws or bolts.

Measuring

Before you can do this, you must first measure the distances over the hoops and transfer this information on to the canvas.

First, mark the centrelines on the front timber and both hoops. Temporarily fix a small screw to the front timber on the centreline, facing the bow. Tie a thin cord around this screw and, supporting the hoops at approximately the right angles, loop the cord once around each hoop on its centreline. Holding the cord quite taut, tie it off at a convenient point on the pushpit rail. The hoops can now be moved forwards or backwards as desired and the looped cord will hold them in position. This is the time to take a careful look at the lie of the hoops and satisfy yourself that they look right as, in the words of many a shopkeeper, 'mistakes cannot afterwards be rectified' (well not easily anyway).

Now for the tricky part. First, carefully measure along the front timber from the centreline outwards and mark off every 300 mm on the timber, until you reach the end. Do the same around each hoop marking each 300 mm from the centreline towards the hinge plate (see sketch). At the ends of the timber and the hoops, the dimension will be smaller than 300 mm.

To help with all the measuring I have included a table in which you can fill in your measurements. This will make transfer to the cloth easier and you will be less likely to make a mistake. I have called all these horizontal measurements (most of which are 300 mm) dimension 'a', with 'a1' being from the centreline to the first mark, 'a2' from the first mark to the second, and so on.

When these dimensions have been recorded,

you can measure the vertical dimensions. From the centreline of the front timber to the centreline of the first hoop will be dimension 'b1'. Record this on the chart and move outward to the first 300 mm mark and measure 'b2', and so on. When all the 'b' dimensions have been recorded, move on to the top panel (i.e. between the two hoops) and proceed to measure all the 'c' dimensions.

Before continuing, it is now necessary to determine the shape and size of the two side panels, which will be triangular in shape. The top of the triangle needs to be about half-way between the hinge plate and the hoop centreline, although some latitude may be necessary to ensure that the top of the triangle is high enough to hold the aft hoop in place but not so high as to restrict the curve. The lower edge of the triangle will need to be shaped to fit the cockpit coaming and should extend towards the stern to give an angle at the top of the triangle of about 30°. Mark these positions temporarily on the cockpit coaming. It will now be possible to determine the 'd' dimensions and record them on the chart.

The chart can be extended to record further dimensions as required. Further diagonal measurements may be taken to ensure the correct shape.

Marking and cutting

You are now ready to mark out your cloth. Remember that you will need hems or tabling unless you are working from a selvedged edge.

Start with the front panel. Draw a straight line 50 mm in from the edge of the material to represent the front timber. Draw the centreline of the panel at right-angles to this line, making sure that there is enough room on either side to accommodate the full width of the panel which is wider at the other edge. Proceed to transfer the dimensions from your chart, working away from the centreline in both directions. Join up these points to reproduce the curved shape and check any diagonal measurements. Next, add on the allowances for the seams and hems (as indicated on the sketch). The front panel may now be cut out.

Marking out the top panel is similar to the front panel except that you have no straight edge from which to work, and so you draw one across the centre of the cloth. The 'c' dimensions are measured off at right-angles to this straight line as before, except that the line is at their mid-point, not one end. Add the allowances for hems etc. Cut the panel out.

Do likewise for the side panels (remember there are two of these), check the diagonals, add the allowances for hems and cut out.

Sewing

The first seam to sew is that between front and top panels. Lay the front panel face up with the 25 mm margin at the top. Place the top panel face down on top of it and ensure that the centrelines correspond and the 25 mm margin on the front panel and the 13 mm margin on the top panel are together. Tack, pin or staple the cloths together. Machine or sew the first seam leaving the appropriate margin (see sketch). Remove the pins or staples and fold the top panel over. Turn the whole thing over so that it lies flat with the inside facing up. Fold the 25 mm wide margin around the 12 mm wide margin and pin or tack stitch to the top panel. Sew the second seam as in the sketch.

Now sew on the two triangular side panels, using the same procedure as above.

With the four panels assembled lay the hood over the frames to check how they fit. They should fit over the frames neatly, with the lower edges overlapping their final positions by about 50 mm. You can now sew up the hems or turnover tabling all round. The hood should now fit snugly and the overlap should be sufficient for the fixing of the turnbuckles or eyelets.

Cut 100 mm wide strips of cloth to make up the pockets (in which the hoops will be fitted later). You will need five short pockets and one long pocket. The lengths are not critical, except for symmetry. The pockets should be machined or sewn in position on the inside as shown on the sketch. Turn in and sew the hems at the end of the pockets before fixing in place. Then turn in the side hems and sew or machine the pockets into position. The long pocket is positioned centrally over the aft hoop. Sew the outer hem back to face first (as you did with the side panel), then fold over and under, turn second inner hem and sew in position.

Fix eyelets or turnbuckles, equally spaced,

around the outer hems. They should be spaced about 150 mm apart ideally, but some variation is necessary to ensure a good attachment at the corners.

Finally, dismantle the plastic tubes from one side only, and thread them through the spray hood pockets. Then re-fasten the plastic tubes with the wing nuts. With a pencil mark through the turnbuckle or eyelet holes on to the cabin, front timber etc. and using this as a centre screw-fix the turnbuckles or lacing hooks in position.

Fitting a window

If you wish to fit a window in your spray hood, it is best done after you have cut out the front panel but before sewing it to the top panel. It is by no means essential to have a window. The kind of clear plastic sheet used is prone to cracking, especially when the hood is folded down onto the cabin top. If you feel, however, that the advantages of having a window outweigh the disadvantages, then you would do well to opt for a simple rectangular shape, as the tabling and stitching required for an oval or round-cornered window is extremely complicated. The example shown on the sketch is for a simple rectangular window which is easy to make and stitch.

With the inside of the front panel facing up, mark on the outline of your window. Cut the clear plastic sheet 24 mm wider and longer than the finished window. Place in position and mark the four corners on the cloth. Next, draw a line 38 mm inside your original window opening, forming a smaller rectangle inside the first. Cut this out and remove the surplus cloth. Then cut the four diagonals from the corners of the rectangle to the corners of the proposed final window opening (see sketch, step 2). Fold back the sides and place the plastic sheet over the top with the corners lining up with the marks. Pin in position and hand sew or machine the first seam; this should be just inside the edge of the plastic. When this is complete, double fold the canvas flap (as shown in step 4 of the sketch) and hand sew or machine a second row of stitches inside the first, close to the edge of the opening.

Distribution Boxes

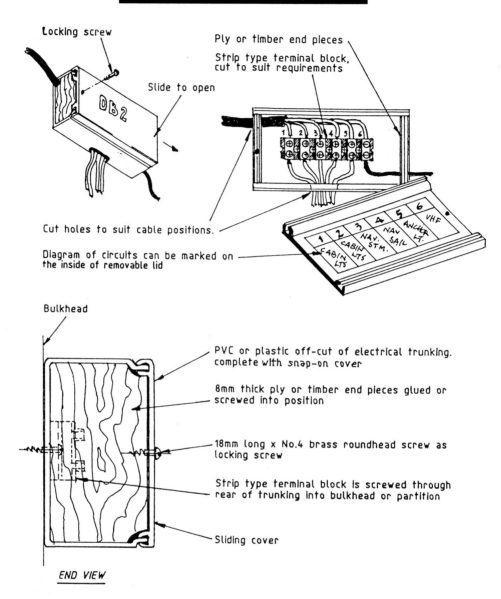

Locking screw

Slide to open

DB 2

Ply or timber end pieces

Strip type terminal block, cut to suit requirements

1 2 3 4 5 6

Cut holes to suit cable positions.

Diagram of circuits can be marked on the inside of removable lid

CABIN LTS / CABIN LTS / NAV. STM. / NAV. SAIL / ANCHR LT. / VHF

1 2 3 4 5 6

Bulkhead

PVC or plastic off-cut of electrical trunking. complete with snap-on cover

8mm thick ply or timber end pieces glued or screwed into position

18mm long x No.4 brass roundhead screw as locking screw

Strip type terminal block is screwed through rear of trunking into bulkhead or partition

Sliding cover

END VIEW

Useful distribution or junction boxes can be made simply from the off-cuts of plastic electrical trunking discarded on many building sites. Cut to the required length and fitted with timber or ply end pieces, they can be fitted almost anywhere on board.

This electrical trunking comes in many widths and depths, and a size should be selected to allow plenty of room to manipulate the cables/wiring inside.

Holes can be drilled in any surface of the box to enable electric wiring to be installed.

These boxes can be used for housing fuses, switches or any other small electrical components.

Tide Clock

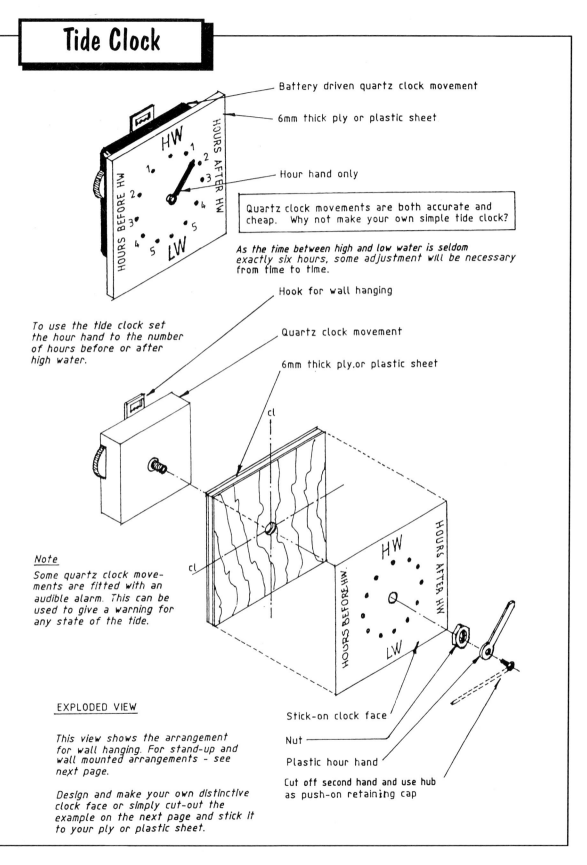

Battery driven quartz clock movement

6mm thick ply or plastic sheet

Hour hand only

HW

HOURS AFTER HW

HOURS BEFORE HW

LW

Quartz clock movements are both accurate and cheap. Why not make your own simple tide clock?

As the time between high and low water is seldom exactly six hours, some adjustment will be necessary from time to time.

To use the tide clock set the hour hand to the number of hours before or after high water.

Hook for wall hanging

Quartz clock movement

6mm thick ply.or plastic sheet

cl

cl

Note
Some quartz clock movements are fitted with an audible alarm. This can be used to give a warning for any state of the tide.

HW

HOURS AFTER HW

HOURS BEFORE HW

LW

EXPLODED VIEW

This view shows the arrangement for wall hanging. For stand-up and wall mounted arrangements - see next page.

Design and make your own distinctive clock face or simply cut-out the example on the next page and stick it to your ply or plastic sheet.

Stick-on clock face

Nut

Plastic hour hand

Cut off second hand and use hub as push-on retaining cap

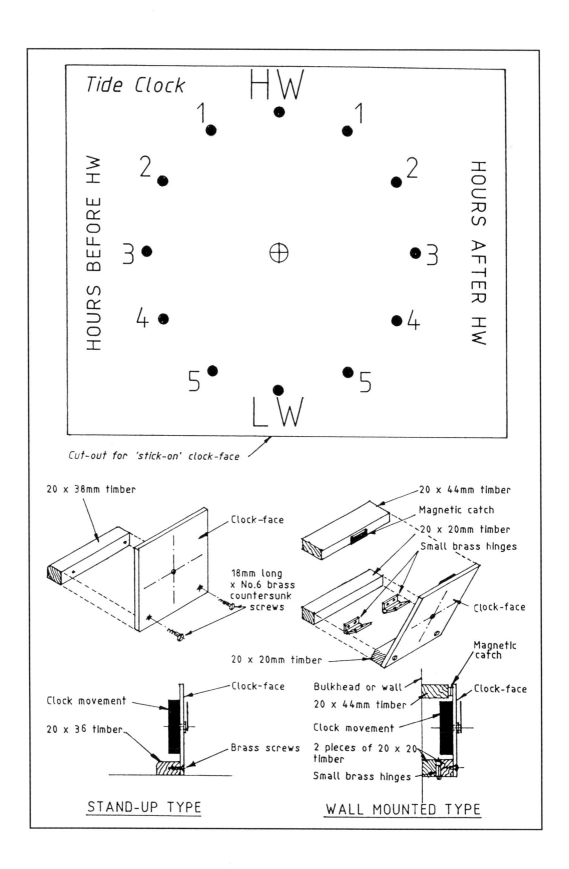

Tide Clock

HW

HOURS BEFORE HW

HOURS AFTER HW

1 1
2 2
3 ⊕ 3
4 4
5 5

LW

Cut-out for 'stick-on' clock-face

20 x 38mm timber
Clock-face
18mm long x No.6 brass countersunk screws

20 x 44mm timber
Magnetic catch
20 x 20mm timber
Small brass hinges
Clock-face
20 x 20mm timber

Clock movement
20 x 36 timber
Clock-face
Brass screws

Bulkhead or wall
20 x 44mm timber
Clock movement
2 pieces of 20 x 20 timber
Small brass hinges
Magnetic catch
Clock-face

STAND-UP TYPE

WALL MOUNTED TYPE

Tide Clock

Materials required

1 × Battery-Driven Quartz Clock Movement (obtainable from Craft Supplies Ltd, The Mill, Millers Dale, Buxton, Derbyshire, SK17 8SN. You will need to specify the shaft length to suit the thickness of your clock face)
1 × set Plastic Clock Hands to suit the above movement
1 × piece 6 mm Plywood, Plastic Sheet or *Traffolite*, approximately 110 mm × 88 mm

Construction

Design your own individual distinctive clock-face on a piece of plain paper. This can incorporate your vessel's name together with any other information you may wish to add. You will need to divide your clock-face into 12 equal segments of 30°. Mark the top point 'High Water' and the bottom point 'Low Water'. Mark the intermediate points on each side from '1' to '5' starting at the top. These are hours either side of high water. You can add 'Slack Water', 'Flood' and 'Ebb' to your clock if you wish.

The design can now be stuck on to a piece of plywood or plastic sheet with a suitable adhesive and protected with a coat of clear varnish. Check that your design will not smudge when varnished (try out a sample beforehand and if smudging occurs try a spray varnish, obtainable from art shops).

Alternatively, you can take your design to an engraver and have it reproduced on *Traffolite*. This is a laminated plastic of two colours, so that when engraved the second colour shows through. The finished result is a two-colour clock-face to your taste. Alternatively, simply cut out the clock-face I have prepared in the sketch and glue this to your backing sheet.

Next, find the centre of your clock-face and drill a hole to take the shaft of your clock movement. Remove the retaining nut from the shaft, fit the clock-face and tighten up the nut. (If you are not hanging the clock up it does not matter if the movement is not in line with the face). Use fibre washers if necessary. Next, take the plastic hour hand and press this into position over the shaft. Then cut the second hand off the hub portion and place the hub over or into the end of the clock shaft. Usually this is simply a press fit. You have no need for the minute hand and this can be discarded. Install the battery and your clock is now ready to use.

As the movement has a built-in hanger on the back, the clock can be hung on the cabin wall from a screw (just like a wall clock, in fact). Should you prefer a different option, you will find a couple of alternatives included in the sketches, but remember to leave enough room for you to be able to replace the battery. Most quartz clock movements run on a 1.5 volt DC MN 1500 battery.

Cockpit Coaming Filler Port

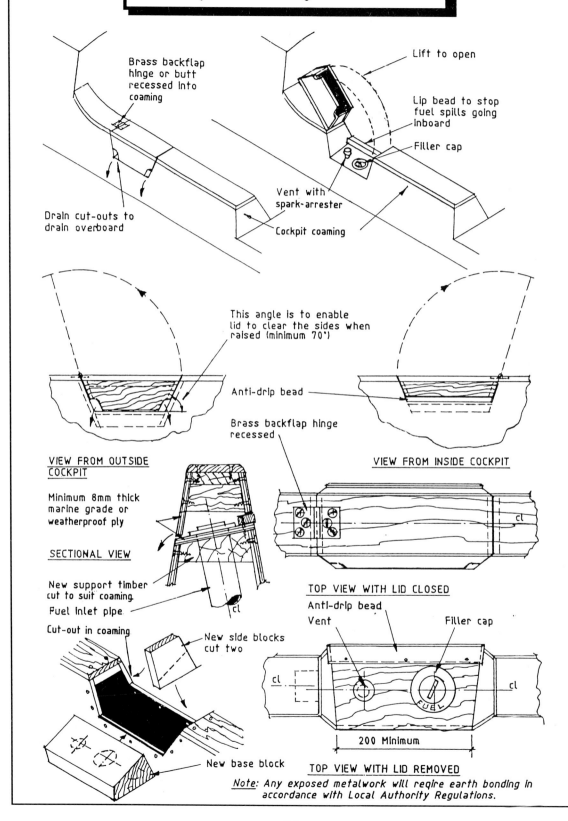

Brass backflap hinge or butt recessed into coaming

Lift to open

Lip bead to stop fuel spills going inboard

Filler cap

Drain cut-outs to drain overboard

Vent with spark-arrester

Cockpit coaming

This angle is to enable lid to clear the sides when raised (minimum 70°)

Anti-drip bead

Brass backflap hinge recessed

VIEW FROM OUTSIDE COCKPIT

Minimum 8mm thick marine grade or weatherproof ply

SECTIONAL VIEW

New support timber cut to suit coaming.

Fuel inlet pipe.

Cut-out in coaming

New side blocks cut two

cl

New base block

VIEW FROM INSIDE COCKPIT

cl

TOP VIEW WITH LID CLOSED

Anti-drip bead

Vent

Filler cap

cl

cl

FUEL

200 Minimum

TOP VIEW WITH LID REMOVED

Note: Any exposed metalwork will reqire earth bonding in accordance with Local Authority Regulations.

Cockpit Coaming Filler Port

Why not fit an enclosed fuel filler port in the cockpit coaming? This raises the filler cap above deck level, lessening the chance for the ingress of water.

Materials required

Some Odd Blocks of Wood of a suitable size to suit your coaming dimensions
1 × Fuel Filler Cap and Tube
1 × Vent Fitting with anti-spark guard
1 × Brass Backflap Butt or Hinge
Screws, Glue and Mastic Sealer as required

Construction

Choose a convenient position on your coaming and mark on the size and shape of your filler port. Make sure that you will have enough room underneath to connect the vent and filler pipes. Note that on the inboard side of the coaming, the depth of the cut-out is less than on the outboard side. This is to provide a sloping base to allow any spilt fuel to drain onto the deck, not into the cockpit. Make sure that at the lifting end (opposite to the hinged end) the angle of the cut will be sufficient to allow the lid to be raised without binding. Using a coping saw or jigsaw, cut out this shape.

Whether your coaming is glass-fibre or timber, you will need to reinforce the lid with end-pieces of ply and glass-fibre, but first let us deal with the hole in the coaming.

Cut some wooden blocks to suit the internal dimensions of the ends of the cut-out. Glue and screw these in place using a good quality sealant, or fibre-glass in position. Next, cut and fit the base block; this will be tapered outwards at the sides and inwards at the ends (see sectional view on the sketch). Cut the base block slightly long as you can tap it down into place with a small hammer or mallet. Glue and screw the base block in position. A marine-grade ply piece can be fixed over the base block with mastic to prevent any leaks occurring through the vertical joints.

Mark the centres for the vent and filler cap and scribe on the circles. Making sure you have left some room at the sides and ends to allow for fitting the anti-drip bead and the lid end supports, drill or cut them out. Fit the vent fitting and the filler cap

in the base block. Connections to the fuel tank can be made with flexible rubber hoses and hose clips, providing the hoses are suitable for use with diesel or petrol. Next, cut and fit the anti-drip bead and screw and glue in place, on the inboard side only.

The base section is now complete and we can now turn our attention to the lid. Try the cut-out lid in position. You will need to trim the inboard edge to fit over the anti-drip bead. If you have fitted a ply overlay to the base block then the outboard edge will need trimming as well. Make sure that the lid, when in place, is flush at the top.

Cut two end blocks to fit inside the lid ends and glue and screw these in position. Check the fit again and plane or sand down until a nice level and flush fit is achieved. Cut out the two lower corners on the outboard side, to allow for drainage.

Put the lid in place and lay the hinge in position. Mark or scribe around it with a pencil or pointer. Measure the depth of the hinge at its thickest and carefully cut out a recess in the lid and the coaming to allow it to sit flush with the top face. Screw the hinge in place with countersunk brass screws. Sand, paint or varnish to complete.

Note

Any metal work in the vicinity of the fuel filling point should be earthed to prevent sparks igniting the fuel. All rubber hoses should be bridged with a suitable earthing wire. If you are unsure about this, seek professional advice.

Emergency Steering

Knot here

Cheek or turning block

Spar

Single block

Rope

Lashing spar to pushpit

Cockpit
Cheek or turning block
See detail 'D'

Single block. See detail 'C'

See detail 'B'

Chain

Rudder

Plate

See detail 'A'

Slot in rudder

ALTERNATIVE BOLT-ON PLATE.

Whipping

3/8 inch or 8mm galvanised chain

Galvanised or stainless steel thimble

12mm diameter rope

DETAIL 'B'

12
14
75
25
20
12
45°

RUDDER SLOT
DETAIL 'A'

'Vee' notched on corners for rope lashing of block

100
12
12

DETAIL 'C'

12mm diameter cheek or turning block

Cockpit coaming

You can use two oars lashed together

Dimension of spar to suit vessel

Minimum gap 150mm

DETAIL 'D'

SPAR SIZING

Emergency Steering

If you have either a stern-hung or under-counter rudder and the tiller or wheel steering mechanism fails, you may be able to rig an emergency steering arrangement as shown on the sketch, provided the rudder is still free to turn.

Materials required

1 x length ³/₈ inch or 8 mm Galvanised Chain, 450 mm long (it may need to be larger for a larger rudder)
2 x ½ inch or 12 mm Galvanised or Stainless Steel Thimbles
2 x ½ inch or 12 mm Single Blocks
2 x ½ inch or 12 mm Turning Blocks or Cheek Blocks. If you have coaming-mounted winches you can use these
1 x Timber Spar, at least 100 mm × 75 mm, length to suit vessel
½ inch or 12 mm diameter Three-Strand or Multiplait Rope
Rope to lash spar in place

Construction

When the boat is out of the water modifications are made to the rudder. If you have a steel rudder, cut a slot in the rear edge as shown in the sketch. If your rudder is of fibre-glass or timber construction, then you can make a slotted plate and bolt this into position. Use at least 6 mm thick mild steel or stainless steel plate and strong bolts as the rudder is subject to considerable stresses. The rest of the arrangement can be made up and stored in case of need.

The ½ inch or 12 mm diameter rope should be cut in half, with one half attached to either end of your length of chain. They can be secured using a metal thimble and a whipping as shown in the sketch or simply tied to the chain with a bowline.

The principle is for the loop of chain to be lowered over the stern of the boat until it is resting against the rear edge of the rudder. The loop is then raised until one or other of the chain links locates in the slot. The links prevent sideways slip and by pulling on one rope or the other the rudder will turn to order. It is important to keep the rope fairly taut or the chain may drop out of the slot. By running the ropes through blocks lashed on either side and tying the ends together in the cockpit, the rudder can be turned by sliding the rope from side to side.

One big snag: if the rope rubs on the side of the vessel the chafing will soon part the rope. To avoid this is will be necessary to guy out the blocks away from the sides of the boat. This can be achieved by a purpose-made spar, notched to take the block lashings, or by lashing oars, the spinnaker pole or even the boat hook over the side to keep the blocks away from the vessel's hull. I would suggest a minimum clearance of 150 mm when the rudder is in the midships position, as when the rudder is turned the rope will move farther away from one side, but closer to the other.

A little experimenting in calm weather to get the system working well may be an advantage, should you ever have to use this emergency steering rig in earnest and in really rough conditions.

Ball and Cone Set

Dimension 'a'

The International Regulations for the Prevention of Collisions at Sea, 1972, states that these shapes shall be black and for vessels of 20 metres length or over:- a BALL shall have a diameter of not less than 0.6 metre; and a CONE shall have a base diameter of not less than 0.6 metre. and a height equal to its base diameter.

In a vessel less than 20 metres in length shapes of lesser dimensions, but commensurate with the size of the vessel may be used.

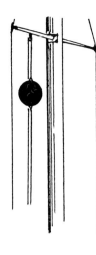

BALL

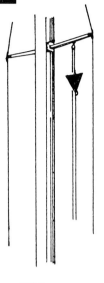

CONE

Your dimension 'a'

Overall length of vessel in metres	dimension 'a'
Under 7	none
7 – 10	200mm
10 – 20	300mm
Over 20	600mm

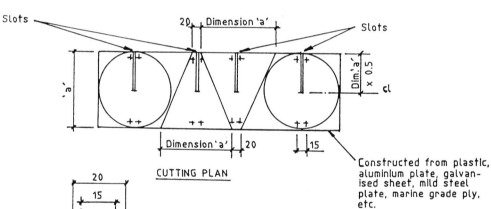

CUTTING PLAN

Constructed from plastic, aluminium plate, galvanised sheet, mild steel plate, marine grade ply, etc.

3mm diameter lacing holes

Slot width to suit thickness of material used

<u>DETAIL FOR DRILLING</u>
<u>LACING HOLES</u>

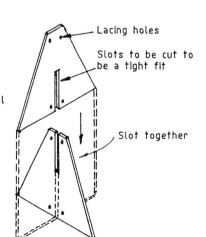

Lacing holes

Slots to be cut to be a tight fit

Slot together

Use 2mm diameter nylon multiplait cord for lacing.

Both these items can be dismantled and folded flat for easy stowage.

Over-Cooker Tray

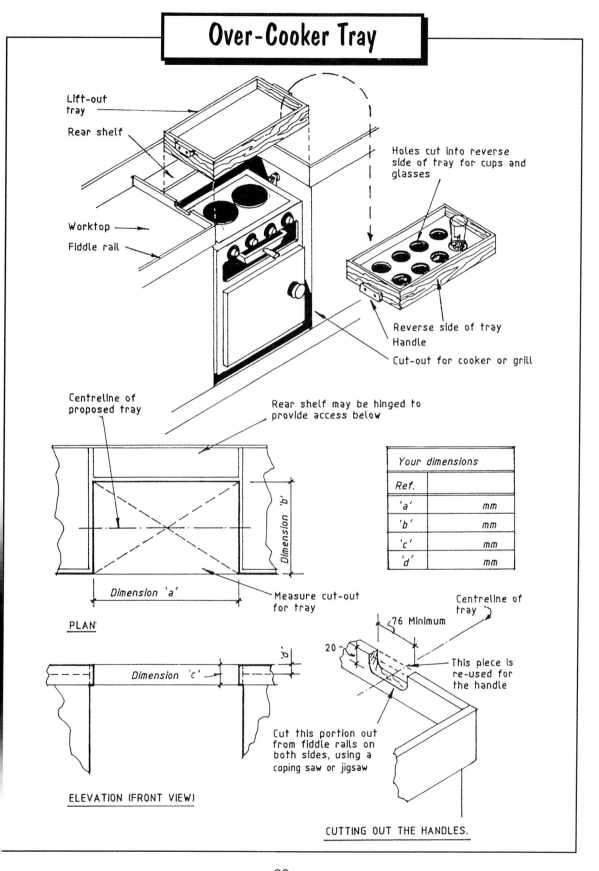

Lift-out tray

Rear shelf

Worktop

Fiddle rail

Holes cut into reverse side of tray for cups and glasses

Reverse side of tray
Handle
Cut-out for cooker or grill

Centreline of proposed tray

Rear shelf may be hinged to provide access below

Dimension 'b'

Dimension 'a'

Measure cut-out for tray

PLAN

Your dimensions	
Ref.	
'a'	mm
'b'	mm
'c'	mm
'd'	mm

Centreline of tray

76 Minimum

20

This piece is re-used for the handle

Dimension 'c'

'd'

Cut this portion out from fiddle rails on both sides, using a coping saw or jigsaw

ELEVATION (FRONT VIEW)

CUTTING OUT THE HANDLES.

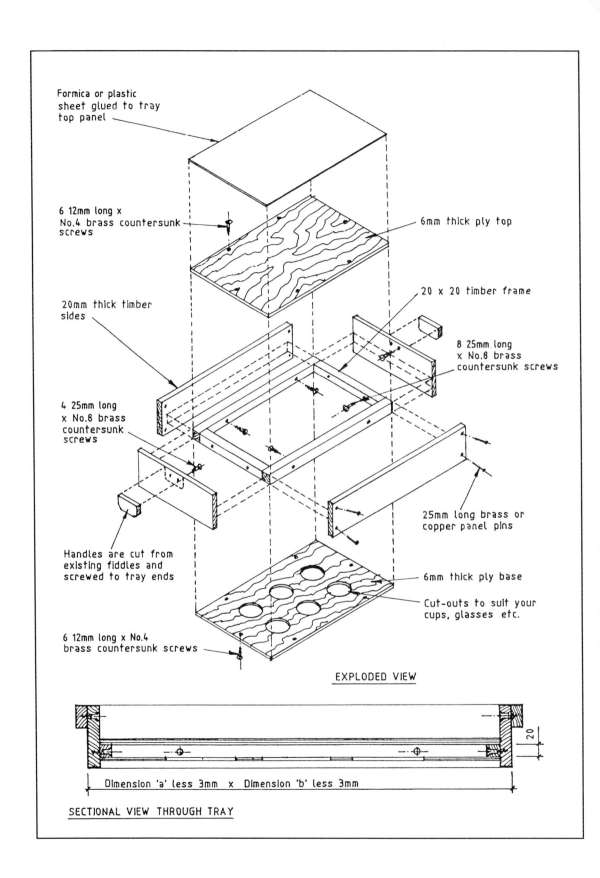

Formica or plastic sheet glued to tray top panel

6 12mm long x No.4 brass countersunk screws

6mm thick ply top

20 x 20 timber frame

20mm thick timber sides

8 25mm long x No.8 brass countersunk screws

4 25mm long x No.8 brass countersunk screws

25mm long brass or copper panel pins

Handles are cut from existing fiddles and screwed to tray ends

6mm thick ply base

Cut-outs to suit your cups, glasses etc.

6 12mm long x No.4 brass countersunk screws

EXPLODED VIEW

Dimension 'a' less 3mm x Dimension 'b' less 3mm

20

SECTIONAL VIEW THROUGH TRAY

Over-Cooker Tray

This over-cooker tray, besides providing additional worktop area in the galley, doubles as a useful non-spill tray for passing drinks up to the cockpit.

Materials required

2 × pieces 6 mm Plywood, dimension 'a' × dimension 'b'
1 × piece Plastic Sheet or Formica, dimension 'a' × dimension 'b'
1 × piece Timber, 20 mm × dimension 'c' × 2('a' + 'b')
1 × piece Timber, 20 mm × 20 mm × 2('a' + 'b')
12 × No 4 Brass Countersunk Screws, 12 mm long
12 × No 8 Brass Countersunk Screws, 25 mm long
8 × Brass or Copper Panel Pins, 25 mm long

Construction

Measure the existing aperture of your cooker, (dimensions 'a' and 'b') and make sure it is square by measuring the diagonals; these should be the same length if the opening is square.

Cut the front and back side pieces of the tray and the front and back frame pieces to the length of dimension 'a' less 3 mm. Glue and screw the frame timber to the front and back side pieces. Next, cut the two end pieces for the tray; these will be as dimension 'b' less the thickness of the front and back side pieces. Cut the frame end pieces the length of dimension 'b' less the two side pieces and the widths of the pieces of the front and back frames. Glue and screw these in position to the end timbers.

Cut the top and bottom ply pieces to fit inside the side timbers. Measure your cups, glasses etc. and cut out circular holes in the base only. Allow a 2 mm gap so that the cups or glasses will not jam in the openings. Glue and screw the ply top and base pieces to the side and ends. Cut and fit a plastic cover or *Formica* sheet to the top side of the tray only, if desired.

Next, mark the centreline position of the tray on the ends and project this mark over the side fiddles. Mark and cut out a section (see sketch) approximately 76 mm long × 20 mm deep. This depth may need to be modified according to the height of the fiddle above the worktop (dimension 'd').

Holding the tray in position with the sides level with the top of the fiddles, mark the position of the cut-outs on the ends of the tray. Take the two pieces you have cut out from the fiddles and glue and screw them in position to the tray ends. This will support the tray and also provide it with handles.

Now, if your tray is square and the handles are fixed centrally it should be possible to turn the tray over and still locate the handles in the slots. It may be necessary to shape the handles slightly to ensure a snug fit. Sand, varnish or paint and you will have a smart reversible tray.

Important note

Remember that the tray must never be placed over the cooker when it is alight or hot as this could cause a fire.

Storage Jars

Large Storage Jars

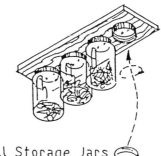

Small Storage Jars

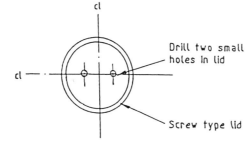

cl

cl

Drill two small
holes in lid

Screw type lid

*Keeps matches and tablets
safe and dry*

Why not utilize your old coffee jars, (or any screw top jar), to provide storage
for any small items you wish to store aboard? Large jars can be used to store
tea, cofee, sugar, rice, flour etc., keeping the contents as dry as possible, while
smaller jars can be used to store screws, bolts, nuts, fuses, matches etc. The
uses are endless.

Simply drill two small holes in each screw lid (both plastic and metal lids are suitable)
and using small brass roundheaded screws, fix to the underside of any convenient
shelf or cupboard.

When the jars are screwed into place they will stay secure in all weathers and
of course, being glass, you can instantly see the contents without having to unscrew
the jar to find out. Glass jars are unfortunately prone to breakage, but they are
cheap and easy to replace.

Typical coffee jar sizes		
Description.	Dimension 'a'	Dimension 'b'
Large	195 to 200mm	90 mm
Medium	150 to 160mm	70 to 76mm
Small	120 to 70mm	50 to 60mm

Dimension 'a'

Dimension 'b'

*By taking your tape measure with you on trips to
the supermarket, you can buy the products in the
size jars that are exactly right for your requirements.*

Jar sizes given are approximate.

Fold-Down Pilot Berth

Pilot berth in folded down position

Lockers, etc.

Setee berth

Cabin sole

Three or four strong brass hinges

20
10
10
20

DETAIL

TOP VIEW

400 Minimum
450
600
2100 Minimum

FRONT VIEW

400   400
50
150
800 Minimum Headroom

Folded mattress

50   'a'

'b'

Holes drilled for drawbolts

'c'

25 x 50 timber

SECTIONAL VIEW
(Where dimension 'a' is greater than dimension 'b'...

Folded mattress

150   'a'

'b'

...or where dimension 'a' is smaller)

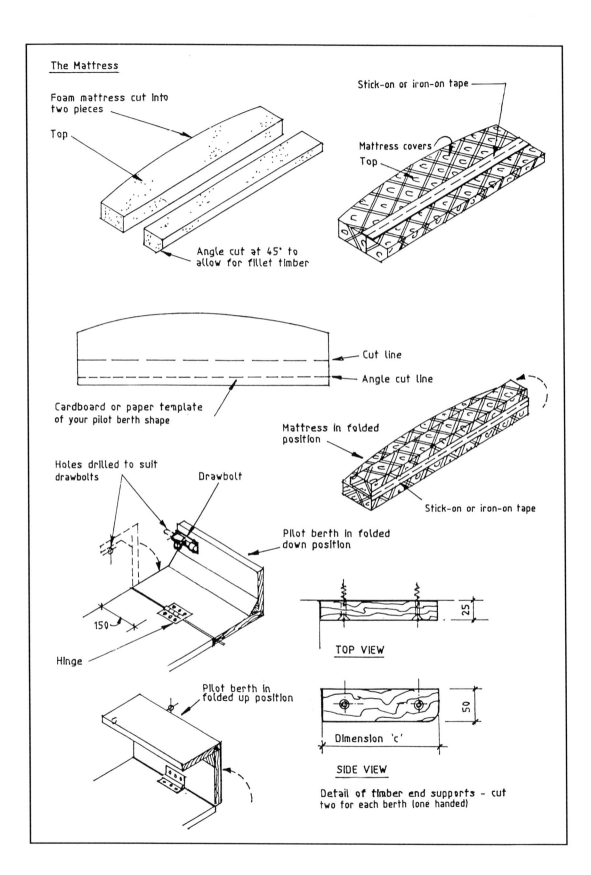

The Mattress

Foam mattress cut into two pieces

Top

Angle cut at 45° to allow for fillet timber

Stick-on or iron-on tape

Mattress covers

Top

Cut line

Angle cut line

Cardboard or paper template of your pilot berth shape

Mattress in folded position

Stick-on or iron-on tape

Holes drilled to suit drawbolts

Drawbolt

Pilot berth in folded down position

150

Hinge

Pilot berth in folded up position

25

TOP VIEW

50

Dimension 'c'

SIDE VIEW

Detail of timber end supports - cut two for each berth (one handed)

Fold-Down Pilot Berth

This extension to the shelf to form a pilot berth is hinged, so that when not in use it can be folded up to allow you to sit on the settee, without getting a crick in your neck.

Materials required

1 × piece 20 mm Plywood or Timber, dimension 'a' × length of berth
1 piece Timber for front, 20 mm × 150 mm × length of berth
1 × 50 mm Timber Fillet, as long as berth
2 × pieces Timber, 25 mm × 50 mm × dimension 'c'
4 × No 10 Brass Countersunk Screws for fixing timber supports to bulkhead, length to suit vessel
3 or 4 × Heavy-Duty Brass Backflap or Butt Hinges, with Brass Countersunk Screws
2 × 6 mm diameter Brass Drawbolts, with Brass Countersunk Screws
16 × No 10 Brass Countersunk Wood Screws, 30 mm long
Cardboard or Paper for template
Foam Rubber Mattress with Mattress Cover
Stick-on or Iron-on Tape

Construction

First, measure your existing shelf width and decide on the extension required to give you a comfortable berth. The dimensions shown are the absolute minimum for an adult. Larger adults may require more width. The materials used will need to be strong enough to support someone climbing in and out of the berth.

It is an advantage to cut the shelf back by about 25 mm in order that, when the berth is folded down, the first 25 mm of the extension will be supported on the shelf frame, as this will prevent bowing when in use.

Cut the 20 mm plywood to the correct width and length. This will form the extension. Allow a gap of approximately 3 mm at either end to make sure that when lifted the extension will not bind on the bulkheads.

Next, cut the front timber and the fillet to the same length. The front board can, if desired, be cut away at the centre to make climbing in and out easier (see sketch). If you decide you would like a cut-out, then this should be done before the timbers are assembled. Assemble the three timbers using marine-grade wood glue and screws.

Next, cut fit and shape the two end bearers or supports and screw or bolt them securely to the bulkheads at each end of the extension. You can now place your assembled extension in the down position resting on the 25 mm ledge and supported by the end bearers.

Taking the brass hinges, mark their position on the extension assembly first. Cut and fix the hinges flush with the top surface of the extension. With the assembly in the down position, mark the position of the hinges on the outer shelf edge. If the shelf thickness is the same as that of the extension, then the shelf must be recessed too. If the shelf is of a thinner material than the extension assembly, then fix the hinges on the surface or pack them up to make the level the same. Fix the inner leaves of the hinges to the shelf.

It now only remains to fix the drawbolts and drill suitable holes to accommodate them. They are fitted to stop the extension falling down on someone's head during rough weather or spilling anything stored there when the berth is not in use. When the drawbolts are locked in place with the extension in the folded position it should be secure enough. When the bolts have been fitted additional holes can be drilled in the folded down position, which will remove any possibility of the extension lifting when in use at sea.

Sand and varnish or paint as preferred.

Mattress

If you look at the arrangement shown in the sketch, you will see that the mattress is formed in two parts. This is to allow it to fold up independently of the extension.

Firstly, make a template of the berth (with the extension folded down). Mark on this template the extent of the trimming required to accommodate the timber fillet and also the line of the cut for dividing the mattress into two parts. Two versions of where to cut the mattress are shown on the sketch. Which one you adopt will depend on the width of the extension (dimension 'a') and the thickness of the mattress when folded over (dimension 'b'). Make sure that when the two halves of the mattress are folded over they do not foul the outer edge of the berth; some adjustment may be necessary should this be the case.

You can now purchase your foam mattress to suit your particular preference as to thickness, quality etc. Cut it in two pieces. A triangular section also has to be trimmed off the bottom of the outside edge along the entire length of the outer piece to accommodate the fillet. Mattress covers are made to fit both pieces of the mattress separately, with zippers if required.

It is now simply a matter of joining the two mattresses together using iron-on or stick-on tape to complete. To do this, put the two mattress parts together and tape the covers together on top. Then fold up the mattress and apply a second length of tape to the inside of the join. Sweet dreams . . .

Floating Workstation

Movable light

Slide

Centre pipe support

Cupboard for screws, bolts, etc.

25mm diameter copper tube rail

Coathanger(s)

Turnbuckle

Hanging space for wet oilies, etc.

Light switch and socket outlet

Tool rack

Tool well

Portable vice (swivel type)

Flap folds down to form full width bench

Wet oilies drain through grating into bilge

Large tool cupboard

Holes drilled in bench top for tools

Position of cupboard above

Tool well

25

Backflap brass hinges

Benchtop

Centreline for coat rail above

450 Minimum.

225

Lift-up flap

70

600

See note *

25

TOP VIEW AT BENCH LEVEL (with flap down)

*Note: This dimension must not be greater than distance from top of bench to clothes rail.

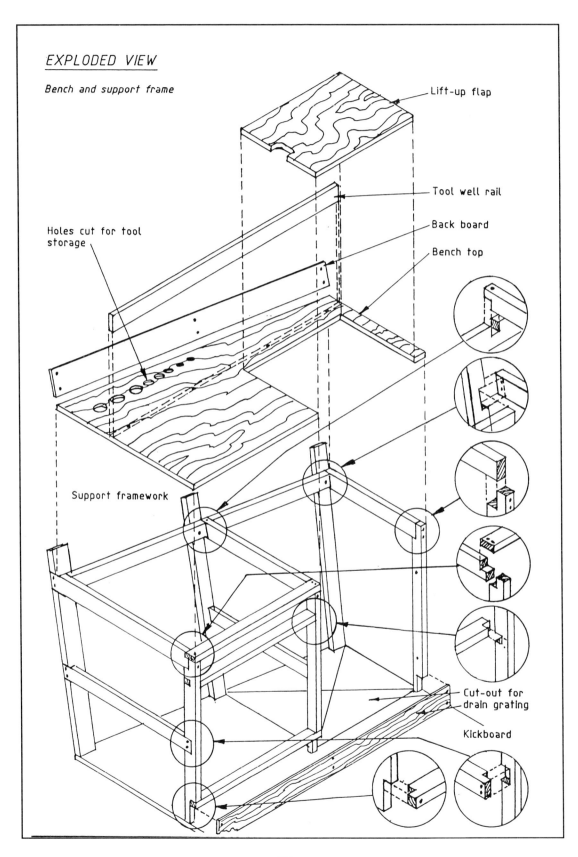

EXPLODED VIEW

Bench and support frame

Lift-up flap

Tool well rail

Back board

Bench top

Holes cut for tool storage

Support framework

Cut-out for drain grating

Kickboard

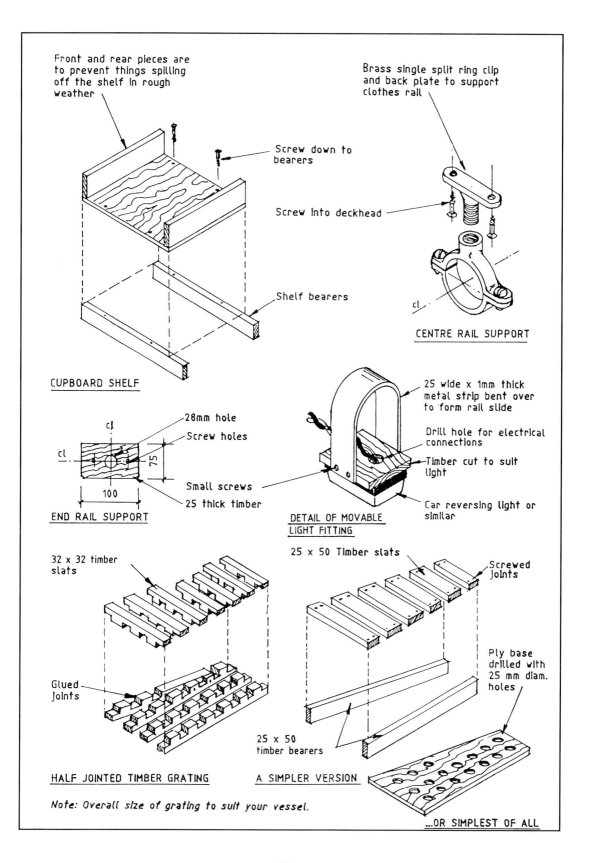

Front and rear pieces are to prevent things spilling off the shelf in rough weather

Brass single split ring clip and back plate to support clothes rail

Screw down to bearers

Screw into deckhead

Shelf bearers

CENTRE RAIL SUPPORT

CUPBOARD SHELF

28mm hole

Screw holes

cl

cl

75

100

Small screws

25 thick timber

END RAIL SUPPORT

25 wide x 1mm thick metal strip bent over to form rail slide

Drill hole for electrical connections

Timber cut to suit light

Car reversing light or similar

DETAIL OF MOVABLE LIGHT FITTING

32 x 32 timber slats

25 x 50 Timber slats

Screwed Joints

Glued Joints

Ply base drilled with 25 mm diam. holes

25 x 50 timber bearers

HALF JOINTED TIMBER GRATING

A SIMPLER VERSION

Note: Overall size of grating to suit your vessel.

...OR SIMPLEST OF ALL

A Floating Workstation

For long-range cruisers, the ability to carry out on-board maintenance work is a great advantage. The floating workstation will make this possible. It can also double as a hanging wet locker. When used as a work bench, the clothes are removed and the flap dropped into position to make a larger work space.

The dimensions of such a bench will depend largely on the space available to you on your vessel and on your individual requirements. The accompanying sketches should, therefore, be used as a guide only and modified to suit your requirements. Consequently, I have not included a materials list for this item, but generally the thicknesses should be as follows:

Bench top: 12 mm to 25 mm
Side panel: 6 mm to 8 mm
Frameworks: 25 mm x 50 mm

Construction

Measure, cut and fit the framework as shown in the sketches to form the bench support. If using the wet locker principle you will need to cut the cabin sole to let water drain into the bilge. The joints shown are meant as a guide only, giving a workable arrangement that only requires a saw and a chisel to achieve. All joints should be secured with brass countersunk screws.

Next, cut and fix the bench top as shown, with its cut-out if you require a wet locker flap. Drill out suitable holes to accommodate chisels, screwdrivers etc. within the tool well area. Using 6 to 8 mm thick ply, cut and fit the side panels and the rear back board. Then cut a suitable timber to length and fix the tool well rail. This can be screw-fixed from underneath the bench top.

The object of the tool well is to provide an area where tools in use will not fall on to the floor in heavy weather, but will stay where they are placed, secure within the tool well.

Any number of shelves can be fitted inside the under-bench cupboard to suit your needs (see sketch for construction). The addition of fronts and backs to the shelves will prevent the contents rolling off and finishing in the bottom of the cupboard.

Next, cut the two end rail supports. Cut and fit the high level rail, which will double as a lamp support and a coat hanger rail. If strong enough it will also serve as a grabrail. Use a brass single ring clip and back plate to support this rail in the middle.

Now construct and fix the grating. There are three alternative versions shown in the sketches. The first is complicated to make, but looks and behaves as a proper grating should. The second, less complicated method is simply to cut slats and secure them to the bearers, leaving gaps of no more than 25 mm in between. The last and simplest method is simply to drill a series of holes in the cabin sole for drainage.

To make a lamp, first obtain a lamp of a suitable voltage. This can often be bought from a car-breaker. Alternatively, a halogen bulb and fitting can be used. You will need a fairly bright light for your workstation (about 25 watts). Having obtained a lamp, you need to attach it to a suitable sliding arrangement. This will have to slide along the clothes rail. If you mount your lamp on a wooden block, this can then be fitted with a loop type strap, to slide along the rail (see sketch). To prevent the flex dropping down and fouling the work bench a few electrician's cable ties loosely fitted around both the cable and the rail will serve. If necessary the flex can be attached to the cable tie with electrician's tape. Lastly, the light needs connecting to the ship's electrical system.

An additional cupboard can often be fitted over the bench for screws, bolts or tool storage. The bench flap and cupboard doors need to be fitted with hinges, cupboard catches and handles.

Finally, fit your bench with a suitable vice; there are many types available. I prefer a clamp-on swivel type engineering vice, which can be removed and repositioned simply, giving the maximum flexibility. Sand, paint or varnish to suit your individual requirements.

Conversion Tables

Length conversion.	
Fractions of an inch to millimetres	
1/16" = 1.59mm	1/2" = 12.70mm
1/8" = 3.18mm	5/8" = 15.88mm
1/4" = 6.35mm	3/4" = 19.05mm
3/8" = 9.53mm	7/8" = 22.23mm

Length conversion. Inches to millimetres	
1" = 25.40mm	7" = 177.80mm
2" = 50.80mm	8" = 203.20mm
3" = 76.20mm	9" = 228.60mm
4" = 101.60mm	10" = 254.00mm
5" = 127.00mm	11" = 279.40mm
6" = 152.40mm	12" = 304.80mm

Length conversion. Feet and inches to millimetres		
1' 0" = 305mm	3' 0" = 914mm	8' 0" = 2440mm
1' 3" = 391mm	4' 0" = 1220mm	9' 0" = 2740mm
1' 6" = 457mm	5' 0" = 1520mm	10' 0" = 3050mm
1' 9" = 533mm	6' 0" = 1830mm	11' 0" = 3353mm
2' 0" = 610mm	7' 0" = 2134mm	12' 0" = 3658mm

Wood Screw sizes		
Size No.	Hole size in inches	Hole size in millimetres
2	5/64"	2mm
4	7/64"	3mm
6	9/64"	4mm
8	11/64"	5mm
10	13/64"	6mm
12	15/64"	6mm
14	17/64"	7mm

Bolt sizes		
Size No.	Hole size in inches	Hole size in millimetres
M2	3/32"	2.6mm
M3	1/8"	3.6mm
M4	3/16"	4.8mm
M5	7/32"	5.8mm
M6	1/4"	7.0mm
M8	11/32"	10.0mm
M10	13/32"	12.0mm
M12	1/2"	15.0mm
M14	9/16"	18.0mm

Standard Timber Sizes			
Rough Sawn		Planed	
Size in inches	Size in millimetres	Size in inches	Size in millimetres
½"	12.5mm	$^3/_8$"	9.5mm
¾"	19mm	$^5/_8$"	16mm
1"	25mm	$^7/_8$"	22mm
1¼"	32mm	$1^1/_8$"	29mm
1½"	38mm	$1^3/_8$"	35mm
1¾"	44mm	$1^5/_8$"	41mm
2"	50mm	$1^7/_8$"	47mm
2½"	63mm	$2^3/_8$"	60mm
3"	70mm	$2^7/_8$"	72mm
4"	100mm	$3^7/_8$"	97mm
6"	150mm	$5^7/_8$"	147mm